Dear Readers,

Before you start this book, I would like the opportunity to share my past experiences, as well as the origin of writing this informative guide.

I was born into a loving, joint, middle class family, and I had a very simple life, from the very start. As I started to grow up, and see the world around me, I saw many things that I wanted to own for myself and provide for my family. However, I didn't have the funds to purchase them. Since then, I kept thinking about different ways to earn money; the word "how" grew and grew in my head and served as a challenge to overcome.

In 1975, my physician told my family and I that I had only six months to live, due to a case of chronic asthma. Like most people, I was not prepared to deal with my death sentence. This news made me think about my priorities- family, friends, goals, etc. During this time, it became clear to me to do what I enjoy and help others with the time that I have left.

Years later, I decided to pursue a very small investment into a soap business. At the time, I was 20 years old and had to research the field quite deeply. That consisted of market (advertising and accounting) as well as product (raw materials and inventory control) research. It is through this background that I gained the perspective of how to start and develop a business, even though I began with no relevant background.

I continued to work and earn money, and decided to move one step forward, and in the early 80's, I started a machine shop manufacturing company, which consisted of auto and defense parts. The progress of the business, however, did not meet my expectations.

10 years later and not discouraged, I started a Mortgage Company. I had to learn everything from the market, by myself. Here, I made my first concrete decision to continue this business at any cost. My hard work paid me back within the year, and in addition, I gained 10 hardworking employees.

During this period, a lot of my clients and friends started to ask me about how to create an LLC, or start a business. After giving advice to friends and family, for over a decade, a colleague suggested that I compile this information into an instructive manual, which could be helpful to people who are starting out the way that I did.

I hope this book will be helpful to you, and others who want to start their own business.

With regards and best wishes,

Kumar Misra

For Consultation:
1104 Rialto Drive, Boynton Beach, FL- 33436
Ph: 561-327-4044, kumarmisra@hotmail.com

ISBN-13:978-1501070228
Library of Congress Control Number: 2014916138
PUBLISHER: CreateSpace Independent Publishing Platform, North Charleston, SC

Copyright © Kumar Misra Boynton Beach Florida 2013

All rights reserved. No part of this publication may be reproduced, stored in a retrieval system or transmitted, in any form or by any means without the prior written permission of the author, nor be otherwise circulated in any form of binding or cover other than that in which it is published and without a similar condition being imposed on the purchaser.

# Introduction

This book is dedicated to those who have a dream to start their own business. People who want to have their own independence day. This book is for those entrepreneurs who have ideas to change their life and make a difference in the world. This book is for those who are tired of working to build someone else's dream. This book is for those who have talent to be their own boss but have not known how to get started. This book is for those who have the dream to create, to develop, to design and to build a product which can help thousands of people to do their job more efficiently. This book is for those who have a dream yet to be fulfilled. This book is for those who want to create a financial freedom, in order to enjoy the life they dream of.

The format of this book is concise, yet informative. Do yourself a favor and write down the ideas you generate while reading. This will allow a broader room for introspection.

Finally, I would like to thank those who have helped me during the creative process, involved in writing this instructional book. First, I would like to thank My daughters, Dr. Neelam Misra, Shipra Misra and Sonali Shukla, In addition, I would like to extend my gratitude to my brother Dr. Ram Misra, my associate Sunil Chaubey and of course, Pam Dwivedi.

## Table Of Contents-

### Chapter-1
Why? ............................................................... 8

### Chapter-2
Idea ................................................................ 12

### Chapter-3
Business Plan ................................................. 16

### Chapter-4
Register Your Company ................................... 32

### Chapter-5
Domain Registration And Social Media ............... 45

### Chapter-6
Financing ........................................................ 51

### Chapter-7
Location Machinery And Equipment ................... 68

### Chapter-8
Goal ................................................................ 74

### Chapter-9
Marketing And Sales ........................................ 80

### Chapter-10
Management .................................................... 93

## Chapter-11
Accounting .......................................................... 99

## Chapter-12
Budgeting And Forecasting ................................ 108

## Chapter-13
Inventory ........................................................... 113

## Chapter-14
Insurance ........................................................... 117

## Chapter-15
Hiring ................................................................ 121

## Chapter-16
Policy And Procedure ........................................ 127

## Chapter-17
Time Management ............................................. 130

## Chapter-18
The Profit .......................................................... 133

## Chapter-19
In Closing .......................................................... 136

# How To Start A Business And Succeed
### -Kumar Misra

# Chapter-1

# Why?

*"The will to win, the desire to succeed, the urge to reach your full potential, these are the keys that will unlock the door to personal excellence"*

-Confucius

Why? Why do you want to start your own business? This is an essential question that you need to ask to yourself. In all honesty, you will probably have more than one answer. Write them down. Most of us have the desire to be our own boss. Said desire, has been around since the beginning of time. We all want, hope and dream of owning our very own businesses. Owning a business gives us pride, fame, success, happiness and a potentially rewarding income. In addition, it gives us the responsibility to meet the financial needs of a company and its employees. During the beginning stages of a business you have to wear many hats: you are the boss, the bookkeeper, the salesman, the worker, the repairman, the janitor and many more. The bottom line is you do whatever it takes to get the job done. Be prepared to work long hours. Every successful business person will tell you that hard work and smart work will pay you dividends once your business gets going.

Again back to the question why? Beneath, I have generated some of the potential answers; you may have come up with:

-I don't like my boss.

-I want to be rich.

-I want the freedom of autonomy.

-I want to be able to spend time with my family.

-I want to make more money.

Take a minute to think about the answers you came up with, as well as what is important to you.

In today's modern society, we are fortunate to have the option to start our own business. There are a plethora of options around us. We are in an age that mankind has dreamt of for centuries. With the rise of technology, we have plentiful opportunities. Never in human history have there been possibilities such as the ones that surrounds us.

Why do you want to start business?

What do you want to get out of a business?

What do you want for your family?

What do you want for your customer?

Consider the answers you came up with. You will find the ignition, which sparks the thoughts of starting a business. A burning desire to start a business is essential to succeed.

Someone once told...

*"if I know how to make a one dollar profit, I will do it a million times and become a millionaire"*

You will need to spend some time to find the answer to why you'd like to start your own business. Once you have the answer, this will be the foundation of your business- what guides you. It will give you a clear picture of what you want from your business. Talk to your close friends and family. Empower yourself with positive thoughts to build your self-confidence. Carry a small diary in your pocket to write down any ideas that come to your mind. It is important to write and revise several times. Think about both the positive and negative aspects of starting a business. How will it change your life, your family life, your social life and your spiritual life? You will be surprised by the answers you will come up with. Your mind is full of answers. Studies have shown that we use only 10% of our brain's potential.

You may come up with answers like the ones listed below:

I want to start business to create a product or a service that I love to do, that I believe in and that I love more than anything else.

I am 100% committed to making this happen.

I want to make money and earn money for me and my family.

I want a steady income and prestige.

I want to create something innovative, to help others.

Go into the clouds, with or without wings. Daydreaming is good for you. Nothing is accomplished without starting out as a dream. If you've got an idea, give it a try. You will be glad you did.

*"If you can dream it you can achieve it"*

*-Zig Ziglar*

# Chapter-2

# Idea

*"First come thought; then organization of that thought, into ideas and plans; then transformation of those thoughts into reality. The beginning, as you will observe, is in your imagination."*

-Napolian Hill

Grab a pen and make a flowchart of your business ideas. Pick one or two that resonate. What is your idea? What kind of business would you like to start? Every year over half a million people start businesses in USA. Some have good ideas and they succeed. Others have faulty ideas and they fail. What makes your ideas unique? Spend a few weeks, months even, to come up with a concrete idea and mission statement. Talk through your ideas out loud. Work through the strengths and weaknesses. Write them down. Once you are confident in your idea, talk to a trusted family member or confidant to get some feedback. Consider the feedback you have received, but be sure to pay close attention to negative feedback. As it will likely force you to rethink your approach and improve upon your original idea.

Although there is pressure to come up with a big idea, remember, most revolutionary concepts started out very small. Today, with the help of the internet, you can search for ideas and inspiration online. Whenever an idea lights up in your mind big or small, write it down. Our thoughts are like dreams, they float away too easily and we forget them the next day.

You do not have to search very far to find a good business idea, most of time it is just around the corner.

Consider this story:

"Once upon a time a farmer had a very large farm. He was making a good living, but he was getting tired of farming. One day a sage came to his home, he told the farmer there is a very shiny stone buried somewhere in the ground and is very expensive. If he can find it, he will be very rich. He will not have to do this hard work, face droughts, floods or other natural disasters that can destroy his crops. The farmer became very curious. After few years he told his only daughter about what the sage had told him. He told her, "Once I get you married to a fine young man, I will sell this land and go look for that bright stone." One day his daughter got married and he sold his land and he went to find that bright stone. The man who bought the farmers land was digging a new well and found dark stone (coal), he started to dig more and there was more coal, during that digging he stumble upon a bright stone which we all know to be a "Diamond!"

The Moral of the story is that opportunities surround us and a good idea can come anytime, anywhere. You may not have to look far and wide to find your golden idea. The best ideas may be just beyond your front door.

Make a List of things you excel at, or enjoy:

Are you good with money?

Are you good at building things?

Are you good at fixing things?

Are you good at creating things?

Just as important, make a contrasting list about things you do not like to do. It may look like this:

I do not like talking with people.

I do not like dealing with finances.

I do not enjoy positions of authority over people.

I do not like to sit at a desk and so on.

What are you good at?

What is your expertise?

Are you good with people?

"To succeed in business, to reach to the top, an individual must know all that there is to know and all that it is possible in that business"

**Business types:**

Here are few types of businesses:

1. Service business

2. Restaurant and food business

3. Manufacturing business

4. Marketing and promotion

5. Sales

6. Advertising

7. Healthcare

8. Construction

9. Consulting

10. Education and training

11. Finance

12. Technology

13. Publishing

14. Franchise business

*"Everyone who has achieved financial independence will tell you that at least in the early days you have to work smarter and harder. The price of success must be paid in fulland it must be paid in advance, there are no shortcuts"*

*-John Cummuta –Author and Financial advisor*

# Chapter-3

# Business Plan

*"Failing to plan is planning to fail"*

First you need to block out time to do business planning. Get out your paper and pencil, laptop or computer. Start writing your plan.

**1. Start with the customer:** Who is your customer, what demographic are you targeting? Think about how your product or service will help the customer. Think of the advantages and benefits to your new customer. Will they feel comfortable working with you?

**2. Research the needs of your customer:** Make sure your plans are well thought out. Make sure your business fulfills the need of your customer.

**3. Have a marketing plan:** Consider your target market, research market conditions. Look into your competitors methods of advertising. Research their promotion campaigns. Research the cost of advertising.

**4. Plan out your expenses:** labor costs, employee costs, payroll taxes. Who will be your key employees? What are their roles in your organization?

**5. Plan out your management:** Team. Specify their roles and responsibilities.

**6. Create a system for everything:** Systemizing will help you duplicate everything you want your customer to have every time. When an individual buys a product/services from you they should know what to expect.

**7. Have financial plans detailed and worked out:** Determine your costs: such as startup costs, operating costs, a revenue generating plan and your profits. This will help you understand your financial situation.

**8. Location:** Plan out the location, physical space and any machinery equipment that may be needed.

**9. Timeline**: Develop a timeline for your plan.

**10. Business Plan:** Prepare good business plan.

## WHY DO YOU NEED A BUSINESS PLAN?

A business plan is road map for your business. A business plan will clarify where you are starting and where you are planning to go. This will show you what it will take to start a business and take it to the next level.

How do you utilize a business plan?

1. A business plan will give you concrete details on what you need to start a business.

2. A business plan is used for raising capital.

3. A business plan is used to hire key people.

4. A business plan is used to get partners.

5. A business plan is used for marketing and promotion.

6. A business plan is used to get credit from the bank.

7. A business plan is used to get credit from your supplier.

For a Successful business plan

-Keep it simple and to the point.

-Keep it brief but thorough.

-Keep in mind that your business is unique.

The following is what should be included in the business plan?

1. Executive summary

2. Mission statement

3. Company description

4. Product and services description

5. Marketing plan

6. Operation and management plan

7. Financial plan

8. Anticipated outcome

## 1. EXECUTIVE SUMMARY:

A Paragraph summarizes your business. This is a summary of your business that is included in the business plan.

## 2. MISSION STATEMENT

What is your mission statement?

A mission statement is a concrete summary of your business goals. Traditionally, these plans are one or two sentences, which reflect the values which drive your company. In addition, they can include the type of business culture you plan on creating.

## 3. COMPANY DESCRIPTION

-Describe the business in detail (1 or 2 pages approx.)

-Describe what product or services you are offering.

-Describe the founders and their experiences.

-Include the business name, location and legal structure.

-Describe machinery, equipment and the human and financial resources.

-Describe your current or projected annual sales.

-Describe the marketing plan.

-Describe your management team.

-Describe your goals and objectives.

-Describe why your business will succeed.

## 4. PRODUCT AND/OR SERVICE

-Describe the product and service you plan to make or sell.

-Describe the uniqueness of your business.

-How does it is compare to other similar products in the market, by parameters, such as price and quality.

-Describe why a customer would patronize your business.

## 5. MARKETING PLAN

-What is your marketing plan?

-Define your target market.

-Describe how people will know about your business.

-Describe your advertising plan.

-Describe how you will compete with other similar businesses.

## 6. OPERATION AND MANAGEMENT PLAN

-Describe briefly your management & operations.

-Describe your plan for hiring.

-Describe your needs for machinery and equipment (leased or purchased).

-Describe your technology requirements.

-Describe any additional requirements.

## 7. FINANCIAL PLAN

-Describe your financial requirements.

-Describe where the funds will come from.

-Describe your contingency plan.

-Describe the accounts receivable and accounts payable.

-Describe the cash flow.

## 8. ANTICIPATED OUTCOME

Describe briefly what your business will look like with a view of the end results. How will it help you, your team, your customers and your investors? Consider also the social and environmental impacts.

### One page Business plan template

1. Executive Summary:

2. Company profile:

3. Describe the business:

4. Marketing and Sales:

5. Management team:

6. Financial Summary:

|  | 1st YEAR | 2nd YEAR | 3rd YEAR | 4th YEAR | 5th YEAR |
|---|---|---|---|---|---|
| INCOME |  |  |  |  |  |
| EXPENSE |  |  |  |  |  |
| NET-PROFIT/ LOSS |  |  |  |  |  |

7. Include an overview of your business plan and your contact information:

### Multipage Business Plan Template

-Your Business Name:

-Address:

-Phone No:

-E-mail:

-Web Address:

-Date:


Table of Contents:


i. Table of contents

ii. Executive summary

iii. Mission statements

iv. Company description

v. Products and services

vi. Marketing plan

vii. Operation and management plan

viii. Financial plan

ix. Anticipated outcome

**Executive Summary**

**Mission Statements**

Company Description

**Products And Services**

**Marketing Plan**

# Operation And Management Plan

**Financial Plan**

Anticipated Outcome

When you are done with your plan, review it with your accountant and other team members before giving it to an outsider.

*"Any idea, plan or purpose may be placed in the mind through repetition of thoughts"*

By. Napoleon Hill

# Chapter-4

# Register Your Company

*"You see things and say why? But I dream things that never were and say why not?"*

-George Bernard Shaw


"LEGAL NAME"

Now that you have completed your business plan, you are ready to name your business. Before you name your business, you need to understand which legal form of business you want. The legal name is very important and you need to know the advantages and the disadvantages of the different types of legal entities. You need to know the tax advantages and legal protections you will have before you decide which legal entity you want to form. You should consult your attorney and/or certified public accountant (CPA) to ensure you are on right track. After all your business represents you, a nice and organized start will be helpful as you move forward.

**There are 2 types of business entities:**

Unlimited Liability

i. Sole Proprietorship or DBA (Doing Business As)

ii. Partnership

Limited Liability

i. C-Corporation

ii. S-Corporation

iii. Limited Liability Co or LLC

**Unlimited Liability:**

In an unlimited liability company such as a sole proprietorship, DBA, or partnership, the owner and partner accept personal and unlimited liability for its debt and obligation. However one of the benefits of an unlimited liability company is being able to avoid paying double taxes on the income you earn.

All the members, stockholders and general partners have a joint responsibility for the company's debts, obligation and liability. This form of entity represents a higher risk than limited liability business entities.

**i. Sole Proprietorship or DBA (Doing Business As)**

This is simplest way to start a business. It is an unincorporated business owned and run by individual with no differences between the business and owner. According to SBA (Small Business Administration) you do not have to take any formal action to form a sole proprietorship, as long as you are the only owner. This situation automatically occurs with business activity. However, you do need to obtain necessary licenses and permits. Regulations vary by industry, state and locality. For more information, go to www.sba.gov and click on the link for licensing and permits.

### DBA (Doing Business As)

If you prefer to start a business under a name, that is not your own name (this is known as fictitious name), you need to file or register a DBA. For example, Debbie Roberts has a cleaning business is called "Clean by Debbie". She can advertise, print business cards and flyers under the fictitious name, "Clean by Debbie". This does require opening a bank account for the business. Every state in the United States has this regulation. However, you need to check with your state or local jurisdiction (such as city and county) for their specific requirements. Corporation and general partnerships can create a DBA with similar requirements. A DBA name is also known as an assumed name or trade name.

### ii. Partnerships

If two or more people start a business together then it is known as a partnership.

There are three kinds of partnerships:

a. General partnership

b. Limited partnership

c. Joint ventures

### a. General Partnership:

In a general partnership, profit, liability and management responsibilities are equally divided among partners. A general partnership must be in writing and must clearly define the role and responsibility of each General and Limited partner.

### b. Limited Partnership:

In a limited partnership there is limited liability, limited responsibility and limited decision making. Limited partnerships must be in writing and filed as such.

### c. Joint Ventures:

A general partner can participate in a joint project for a limited period of time or work on a single project. It can be ongoing if the venture continues and must be filed as such.

One of the advantages of partnerships is that, partnerships do not pay taxes on their income, but it passes the tax burden on to all of the partners. Partnerships must use IRS form 1065 to report its income or profit/loss to the IRS. Additionally, each partner will file schedule K-1 for income or loss.

### Limited Liability:

### Corporation:

Corporations organize and file with their state for registration. Corporations act as an individual, independent legal entity that is owned by its shareholders. Corporations enjoy most of the rights and responsibilities that individuals have. A corporation has the right to enter into contracts, borrow money, hire employees, own assets and file taxes.

One of the most important benefits of a corporation is limited liability. Shareholders participate in the profits, but are not held personally liable for the corporation's debts.

There are profit corporations, which is started to make money. There are also non profit corporations created for charitable work or as an entity of religious organizations such as churches or temples.

I.C- Corporation or C-Corp: Is the most common type of corporation. It provides limited liability to its owner which we call a shareholder.

C-Corp files one tax return with the IRS using form 1120.

II.S-Corporation or S-Corp: Provides the same limited liability as C-Corp to its shareholders or owner, however the S-Corp does not pay taxes at a business level. They file information as federal tax return (IRS form 1120 S) but no income tax is paid on corporate level income and losses are passed down to the owner. The owner must file in his/her own personal tax return and any tax due is paid by individual owner.

Limited Liability Company= "LLC"

Limited Liability company or LLC is somewhat similar to a partnership, but it has legal protection of its personal assets similar to a corporation. It must be registered with the state and must file articles of organization with the secretary of state. LLC is much less formal than a corporation.

Unlike shareholders in a corporation, LLC's are not taxed as a separate business entity instead it passes the profits and losses to its members.

*"Happiness is not something you postpone for future, it is something you design for present"*

-Jim Rohn

## NAMING YOUR COMPANY

Finding the right name for your company is of the outmost importance. With a clever, creative name you can make your self the talk of the town by standing out. In contract, the wrong name can pigeonhole you as just another business, without anything special to offer. You need to put as much effort in naming your business as you did for the idea of the business or the planning for your business.

In addition, Your company name should convey the values and uniqueness of your product and company. You need to do research to come up with a attention-grabbing name. You also need to check the availability of that name with the secretary of state. Be sure to check the availability of the name for the domain name of your website. The name will be a reflection of your company and also you as the owner.

**THE FOLLOWING ARE A COMPREHSIVE LIST OF TIPS TO KEEP IN MIND.**

-When you are naming your company, you are creating the identity of your brand.

-First impression is the key. Remember that you are selecting potential name.

-Create a name that is both simple & meaningful. You should not have to explain the meaning of your company to those who meet.

-Spend time at the beginning, thinking about the one thing you would like your company to do. Who are your customers? Who are your competitors? Asking these questions will help you come up with a meaningful name.

-Naming a company is like naming a baby. How will the name sound when people pronounce it? How will the domain name sound in comparison to other domain names out there?

-Let your name tell a story.

-Make sure you really love the name.

**REGISTER YOUR BUSINESS**

Once you have established the company name, it is time to register your company. You can go to your state's website or if you would like to register in a different state you can check with that state for the availability of the name.

Requirements and costs to register: Check not only the cost to register, but also the cost of renewal every year. Also if you register in a different state you need a register agent.

## WHAT IS A REGISTER AGENT?

A register agent provides the address of your business to state and/or local authorities. These register agents charge a fee to provide you the address and at the same time take care of the annual filing and renewal paperwork.

You can find all the information you need online.

If you register a corporation you need an article of corporation, which you can buy online. If you register a LLC, you need an organization paper. If your company is a partnership you need a partnership agreement.

## FEDRAL TAX ID NUMBER:

The next thing you need after registering your company as a corporation is a Federal Tax Id Number or EIN (Employer Identification Number) you can apply at the IRS website www.irs.gov and get the number, in some cases you can register and get the EIN almost immediately.

**BUSINESS LICENSE:**

Depending upon the type of business, you may need a license from the federal, state or local government. In some businesses you need a license immediately. In some businesses you can wait to see if your business takes off. For example, if you are opening a bar, you need a liquor license first. If you are selling products or services online from your home, you can wait a bit to see if your business is succeeding before applying for a business license.

*"If you don't build your dream, someone else will hire you to help them to build theirs"*

-Dhirubhai Ambani

## STATE CORPORATION OFFICES

| | | |
|---|---|---|
| ALABAMA<br>PHONE: 334-242-5324 | BUSINESS SERVICE | RSA Union Building<br>100 N UNION STREET<br>MONTGOMERY, AL-36130 |
| ALASKA<br>PHONE: 907-465-2974 | CORPORATIONS, BUSINESS AND PROFESSIONAL LICENSING | 333 WILLOUGHBY AVENUE, JUNEAU, AK-99801-1770 |
| ARKANSAS<br>PHONE: 501-682-3409, 501-682-1010 | BUSINESS/ COMMERCIAL SERVICE | 1401 WEST CAPITOL AVE, STE 250<br>LITTLE ROCK, AR-72201 |
| ARIZONA<br>PHONE: 602-542-3026 | CORPORATION COMMISSION | 1300 W. WASHINGTON $1^{ST}$ FLOOR PHOENIX, AZ-85007-2929 |
| CALIFORNIA<br>PHONE: 916-657-5448 | BUSINESS PORTAL | P.O BOX 944260, SACRAMENTO CA-94244-2600 |
| COLORADO<br>PHONE: 303-894-2200 | BUSINESS CENTER | 1700 BROADWAY DENVER, CO- 80290 |
| CONNECTICUT | COMMERCIAL RECORDING DIVISION | Office of the Secretary of the State<br>State of Connecticut<br>30 Trinity Street<br>Hartford, CT 06106<br>Telephone: (860) 509-6200 |
| DELAWARE<br>PHONE: 302/739-4111 | DIVISION OF CORPORATIONS | Division of Corporations<br>Bldg.401 Federal Street, Suite 4, Dover, DE 19901 |
| D C<br>PHONE: 202-442-4400 | CORPORATIONS DIVISION | 1100 $4^{TH}$ STREET S. W, WASHINGTON, DC- 20024 |
| FLORIDA<br>PHONE: 850-488-9000 | DIVISION OF CORPORATIONS | 2661 EXECUTIVE CENTER CIRCLE TALLAHASSEE, FL-32301 |
| GEORGIA<br>PHONE: 404-656-2817 | CORPORATIONS DIVISION | 2 MLK. JR. DR., SUITE 313 FLOYD WEST TOWER, ATLANTA, GA- 30334-1530 |
| HAWAII<br>PHONE: 808-586-2744 | BUSINESS REGISTRATION DIVISION | P.O BOX 40 HONOLULU, HAWAII - 96810 |
| IDAHO<br>PHONE: 208-334-2301 | BUSINESS ENTITIES DIVISION | PO Box 83720<br>Boise ID 83720-0080 |

| | | |
|---|---|---|
| ILLINOIS<br>PHONE:888-261-5112 | BUSINESS SERVICES DEPARTMENT | 213 STATE CAPITOL<br>SPRINGFIELD<br>IL-62756 |
| INDIANA<br>PHONE: 317-232-6576 | CORPORATIONS DIVISION | 302 W. WASHINGTON ST., ROOM E018 , INDIANAPOLIS , IN-46204 |
| IOWA<br>PHONE: 515-281-5204 | BUSINESS SERVICES DIVISION | $1^{ST}$ FLOOR, LUCAS BUILDING 321E $12^{TH}$ ST., DES MOINES, IA-50319 |
| KANSAS<br>PHONE: 785-296-4564 | BUSINESS ENTITIES | 120 S.W $10^{TH}$ AVE TOPEKA, KS-66612-1594 |
| KENTUCKY<br>PH: 502-564-3490 | BUSINESS SIRVICES | 700 CAPITAL AVE., SUITE 152, FRANKFORT, KY-40601 |
| LOUISIANA<br>PHONE: 225-925-4704 | CORPORATIONS SECTION | P.O. Box 94125, Baton Rouge, LA 70804-9125 |
| MAINE<br>PH: 207-624-7736 | DIVISION OF CORPORATIONS | 101 STATE HOUSE STATION, AUGUSTA, MAINE- 04333-0101 |
| MARYLAND<br>PHONE: 410-767-1184 | BUSINESSES – TAXPAYER SERVICES | 301 W, PRESTON ST. BALTIMORE M.D 21201 – 2395 |
| MASSACHUSETTS<br>PHONE:617-727-7030 | CORPORATIONS DIVISION | 220 MORRISSEY BLVD BOSTON , MA 02125 |
| MINNESOTA<br>PHONE:877-551-6767 | BUSINESS PORTAL | 60 EMPIRE DR SUITE 100 SAINT PAUL, MN 55103 |
| MICHIGAN<br>PHONE: 517-241-6470 | CORPORATION DIVISION | P.O. BOX 30054<br>LANSING, MI 48909 |
| MISSISSIPPI<br>PHONE: 601.266.4137 | BUSINESS SERVICES | Forrest County Hall (FCH) 101 118 College Drive #5133 Hattiesburg, MS 39406 |
| MISSOURI<br>PHONE:573-751-4936 | BUSINESS PORTAL | 600 W MAIN ST. JEFFERSON CITY, MO 65101 |
| MONTANA<br>PHONE :406-444-2034 | BUSINESS SERVICES | 1301 E $6^{TH}$ EVENUE , HELENA MT 59601 |
| NEBRASKA<br>PHONE :402-477-4079 | BUSINESS SERVICES | P.O BOX 94608<br>LINCOLN , ME, 68509-4608 |
| NEVADA<br>PHONE:775-684-5708 | COMMERCIAL RECORDINGS DIVISION | 202 NORTH CARSON STREET CRASON CITY , M V , 89701 |

| | | |
|---|---|---|
| NEW HAMPSHIRE PHONE:603-271-3246 | CORPORATIONS DIVISION | 107 NORTH MAIN STREET , CONCORD, MH 03301-4989 |
| NEW MEXICO PHONE:505-827-3619 | CORPORATIONS BUREAU | 325 DON GASPAR, SUITE . 300 , SANTA FE , NM 87501 |
| NEW YORK PHONE: 518-473-2492 | DIVISION OF CORPORATIONS | 123 WILLIOM STREET , N.Y – NY 10038-3804 |
| NORTH CAROLINA PHONE: 919-807-2225 | DIVISION OF CORPORATIONS, STATE RECORDS AND UNIFORM COMMERCIAL CODE | 2 SOUTH SALISBURY STREET , RALEIGH , NC 27601-2903 |
| NORTH DAKOTA PHONE: 701-326-4284 | BUSINESS REGISTRATIONS | 600 E BOULEVARD AVENUE DEPT 108 BISMARCK ND 58505-0500 |
| OHIO PHONE: 614-644-6889 | BUSINESS SERVICES | 180 EAST BROAD STREET , 16$^{TH}$ FLOOR, COLUMBUS OHIO - 43215 |
| OKLAHOMA PHONE: 405-521-3771 | BUSINESS SERVICES | 2300 N. LINCOLN BOULEVARD , STE , 101OKAHOMA CITY, OK. 73105-4897 |
| OREGON PHONE: 503-986-2200 | CORPORATION DIVISION | 255 CAPITOL ST NE STE 151 , SALEM OR-97310-1327 |
| PENNSYLVANIA PHONE: 717-787-1057 | CORPORATION BUREAU | 401 NORTHSTEREET R00206 , HARRISBURG PA – 17120 |
| RHODE ISLAND | CORPORATION DIVISION | 148 West River Street Providence, RI 02904-2615 Ph:401 222-2185 Fax:401 222-1309 |
| SOUTH CAROLINA PHONE: 803-734-2158 | BUSINESS FILINGS | 1205 PENDLETON STREET , SUITE 225 COLUMJIA SC 29201 SC |
| SOUTH DAKOTA PHONE:605-773-3537 | CORPORATIONS | 500 EAST CAPITOL AVENUE , PIERRE SD 57501-5070 |
| TENNESSEE PHONE:615-741-2286 | DIVISION OF BUSINESS SERVICES | 6$^{TH}$ FLOOR TOWER , NASHVILLE , TN 37243-1102 |
| TEXAS PHONE:512-463-5555 | CORPORATIONS SECTION | P.O BOX 13697, AUSTIN , TEXAS-78717 |

| | | |
|---|---|---|
| UTAH<br>PHONE:801-530-4849 | DIVISION OF CORP. & COMMERCIAL CODE | P.O BOX 146705 SALT LAKE CITY UTAH 84111 |
| VERMONT<br>PHONE: 802-828-2386 | CORPORATIONS | 128 STATE STREET, MONT PELIER VT 05633-1104 |
| VERGINIA<br>PHONE: 804-371-8230 | BUSINESS INFORMATION CENTER | 1220 BANK STREET, $3^{RD}$ FLOOR SOUTH RICHMOND, VA 23219 |
| WEST VIRGINIA<br>PHONE:304-558-6000 | BUSINESS ORGANIZATIONS | 1900 KANAWHA BLVD EAST CHARLESTON, WV, 25305-0770 |
| WASHINGTON<br>PHONE:360-725-0377 | CORPORATIONS DIVISION | P.O BOX 4023, OLYMPIA WA 98504-0234 |
| WYOMING<br>PHONE:307-777-7377 | CORPORATIONS DIVISION | THE CAPITOL BUILDING .200 WEST $24^{TH}$ STREET, CHEYENNE, WY – 82002 |

# Chapter-5

# Domain Registration And Social Media

*"The difference between a successful person and others is not a lack of strength, not a lack of knowledge, but rather lack in will"*

-Vince Lombardi

**DOMAIN:**

Create a domain name on the Internet. The domain name is comparable to an address. This will provide the platform for your customer to find you. For example, if you register www.mycompany.com, potential clients can find your company, your product and services with greater ease.

**Register your domain:**

You must register your domain. There are a number of companies to choose from, such as www.godaddy.com, www.1and1.com, www.register.com, www.yahoo.com and many more.

When you are selecting a company to register your website, check the cost of registration, the renewal cost and the hosting cost. Find out what other benefits are offered when working with a specific company. For example, do they have a website design or software included in their package? Do they have search engine optimization? What kind of internet security do they have?

**Hosting:**

Once you register your domain name, you need someone who can host your website on their server. This could be the same place where you registered your domain or you could choose a different company to host your website. There are many companies providing hosting services. Most of the companies have multiple hosting packages to choose from. They will provide an e-mail address for you and your company on their server.

**Before you finalize, find out;**

A. What kind of internet security do they have?

B. Do they provide business verification?

C. Do they provide virus scans, spam scans, display card for your site, a secure data center and network scanning?

D. What kind of support do they have? 24X7? Phone, email, chat tutorial or online help?

E. What kinds of marketing support do they have? Do they offer any credits for Adwords, Yahoo, Bing or other similar companies?

F. Do they have site analytics software? Website authentication?

G. What type of web design support do they have?

H. Do they have a blog template, photo gallery or other templates such as a basic web builder?

I. Find out how much storage space they will provide for your website.

**E-commerce:**

If you're planning to make a sale online and/or collect money online then you need to have an e-commerce account on your website. Find out the cost to initiate an e-commerce account and the monthly or per transaction cost. What type of credit or debit cards do they accept from customers? Will you opt. to use services such as Paypal?

**SOCIAL MEDIA**

**What is social media?**

Social media is a media intended for social interaction, using a highly accessible communication and publishing format. People can create, share and exchange ideas and information in virtual communities on the internet. Social media on the web takes on many different forms, such as internet forums, blogs, podcasts and apps.

**Why social media is important?**

A very large number of people have access to computers, smart phones and tablets. They spend more time on their devices, than they do watching TV or reading printed media (newspapers or magazines).

Social media sites, such as Facebook have millions of people logged on at any given moment sharing ideas. As a business owner, you can have your product and services at the attention of these people at almost no cost to you. Therefore, you must have your company on a social media platform. This will give you lot of exposure with a little to no cost.

**Popular social media:**

-Facebook

-Linkedin

-Myspace

-Twitter

-Youtube

-Flicker

-Pinterest

-Instagram

-Snapchat

**1. Blog:**

You may decide to create a blog for your company. A blog can be a beneficial space, where you can post relevant articles about your business (pro-tips) and upcoming projects. Remember, your personal blog should not have an overwhelmingly commercial tone. You want your audience to relate to it on a variety of levels. That's not to say that you should include information about your personal life, but you are not limited to a single, specific topic. .

**2. Facebook and Google plus:**

You can also create a business account with networking sites like Facebook or Google plus. Again, keep the business account separate from your personal account.

**3. Linkedin:**

Within the last decade, LinkedIn has inarguably become one of the most important social networking sites, for both professionals and businesses. Having your business profile on LinkedIn allows your target audience to find your product and company with ease.

**4. Twitter:**

You can create a business account on Twitter. Twitter allows you to broadcast information about your business in 140 characters or less. You can include anything from tips and lifehacks, to customer service, or even graphics.

### 5. Youtube, Flicker and Pinterest:

You can create an account on sites such as Youtube, Flicker or Pinterest for your business. Here you can post your marketing videos, photos and slides. You can even post a Powerpoint presentation about your business.

Remember, social media is like advertising without the expense. You can get lots of exposure for free. In today's technologically driven work-sphere, it would be a squandered opportunity to not take advantage of such a tool.

*"To succeed in business, to reach the top an individual must know all that it is possible to know about their business"*

*-J Paul Getty.*

# Chapter-6

# Financing

*"Always do your best, what you plan now you will harvest later"*

*-OQ Mandino*

Now, how will you finance this venture? Once you have your business idea ready to go, the next step is figuring out how to finance your business idea. Where will the money come from?

Before we talk about financing your business, let me explain the types of loans available. Once you understand the terminology, it will be easier for you to understand the methods, process and availability of these loans. Further more, you will understand the advantages and disadvantages of the different kinds of loans.

**Types of loans:**

1. Line Of Credit Loan

2. Installment Loan

3. Fully Amortized Loan

4. Balloon Loan

5. Secure Loan

6. Unsecure Loan

7. Interim Loan

8. Letter Of Credit

9. Short Term Loan

10. Long Term Loan

11. Inventory Loan

12. Personal Guaranteed Loan

13. Accounts Receivable Loan

14. Working Capital Loan

15. Credit From Supplier

16. Equipment Financing

**1. Line Of Credit Loan:**

A line of credit is a credit given to a business or individual by a bank or financial institution. This is a good source of money that can easily be tapped into as needed. Interest is paid on the money withdrawn. This is also known as a revolving line of credit.

**There are 2 types of line of credit loans:**

### (a) Secure line of credit:

This is a line of credit on your home or business. It is secured by your home or business assets.

### (b) Unsecured line of credit:

Unsecured lines of credit include charge cards and personal lines of credit. This is based on your creditworthiness and income.

## 2. Installment Loan:

In an installment loan, you make a set number of scheduled payments over a period of time. Examples include: car loans and home mortgages. The payment amount is set, unlike charge cards where there is a revolving payment (With charge cards the monthly payment is variable).

## 3. Fully Amortized Loan:

An amortized loan is a pre-schedule payment of interest and principal. Your amortized loan payment is calculated based upon the number of years. For example, a 30 years fixed mortgage is amortized over 30 years as 360 equal payments.

### 4. Balloon Loan:

With a balloon, the loan will "balloon" over a set period of time. What that means is, that you will make small monthly payments and at the end of the term of the loan, the full balance is due. For example if you have a 5 years long balloon loan with 30 years amortization. You make 59 payments based on 30 years amortization and at the 60th payment, you pay the balance due. Alternatively, you may make interest payments in 59 installments and at the last payment (60th) you pay the principal loan. This is also called a bullet loan.

### 5. Secure Loan:

Any loan secured by fixed assets, such as real estate, stocks and bonds, Certificates of deposit, the cash value of insurance, machinery and equipment.

### 6. Unsecure loan:

A loan which is given to you based on your creditworthiness. This can be from your bank, your supplier or from a private individual.

### 7. Interim Loan or Bridge Loan:

A short term loan made to a company or individual until long term financing is in place.

**8. Letter Of Credit:**

A letter from a bank or financial institution guaranteeing payment to the seller of goods and services made upon satisfactory delivery of such goods and services. A letter of credit is mostly used in international transactions.

**9. Short Term Loan:**

A loan which is made over a short period of time is known as a short term loan. This loan could be from 1 week to 3 years. Some examples of short term loans include: payday loan, bridge loan and green loan.

**10. Long Term Loan:**

A long term loan is a loan which is made for a longer period. It can have a duration lasting from 3 years to 30 years. Long term loans carry lower payments, which is important because that gives the business a great cash flow.

**11. Inventory Loan:**

A loan made against current inventory of goods.

**12. Personal Guaranteed Loan:**

In this type of loan you may have to give a personal guarantee in addition to your business guarantee. Most of Small Business Administration loans require personal guarantees.

### 13. Accounts Receivable Loan:

This is also known as invoice factoring, where you borrow against your accounts receivable. This is a short term loan. Suppose your customer pays you in 30 to 90 days, but you need money sooner than that. You can get an accounts receivable loan until you get paid from your customer. You pay this loan back using the money you receive from your customer.

### 14. Working Capital Loan:

A loan made to pay payroll, utilities, buy supplies, pay rent and pay the monthly obligations to run a business. This is unsecured financing. This loan gives you operating liquidity.

### 15. Credit From Supplier:

This is a credit line you get from your supplier for buying their product. In beginning, it can be difficult to get credit from your supplier, but as your business grows, you can get all the raw materials and supplies on credit from your supplier. This credit is good for 30 to 90 days.

You pay your supplier as you receive your money from your customer. This is an ongoing process.

**16. Equipment Financing:**

Most of the time, you can finance your machine and equipment from the machinery dealer, bank or finance company. This is similar to fixed assets financing. Generally the financing terms are for 2-10 years. This is a good way to get money to finance the equipment requirements for your business.

*"Destiny is no matter of chance, this is a matter of choice, it is not a thing to be waited for, but a thing to be achieved"*

-William Jennings Bryan

**Sources of Funding**

I. Self Financed

II. Family And Friend

III. SBA Loan

IV. Government Loans And Grants

V. Venture Capital

VI. Joint Venture

VII. Private Lender

VIII. Private Investor/Silent Partner

IX. Partnership

**I. Self-Finance:**

You'll need to work on self-financing. Ask yourself questions, such as "How much money can I come up with, by myself?" Begin by making a list of your assets and liabilities to see what your actual net worth is. Next, look at your liquid assets, such as money in the bank, savings account, money market loan and/or stocks and bonds. Finally, find out how much you can invest in your business without compromising your standards of living.

Real Estate:

If you own real estate, consider taking a line of credit before starting a business. Alternatively, think about refinancing your home to take some equity out. Once you start your business, you will be considered self-employed and unfortunately, no bank will give you a loan until you have been in business for at least two years. Until then, you cannot refinance your home or get a line of credit. This is a very important consideration and you must carefully plan out your finances. It could be months, or even a year before money starts to come in from your business. You will need to downsize your standard of living until your business generates positive cash flow.

Charge Card:

A charge card (credit card) is an alternative option for financing part of your business. However, it can be costly. Financing your venture using a charge card is a possibility, however it isn't always successful. I once had a client who wanted to buy a business. One year before making the purchase, he started applying for credit cards. He tried to get as many as he could. Since his credit and income were very good, he had over 30 charge cards and each one of those had cash advances from $5000 to $20,000. He was able to raise over a half a million dollars in equity and successfully paid off all of his charge cards once the business started to make money. If you are planning this route to raise money, then find credit cards with low interest rates and maximum cash advances. As I have mentioned, you will have to plan this out with extreme care; an unfortunate outcome could potentially include a debt with a high interest rate and high frequent payments.

Sell assets that you own:

Check to see if you have assets to sell. For example, if you have land you can sell it and get some cash from the sale. If you own a boat you can sell it and raise funds. If you own an extra car you can sell it as well. Check around for any of valuable assets that you have but you are not using, you can get a loan against high ticket items or sell them to raise some cash.

401 K, IRA:

If you have 401 K you may be able to get some cash in advance to start up a part time business. Generally you are allowed up to 50% of your cash value. You must check with your employer or 401 K provider for details.

Some states allow you to withdraw from your IRA as long as you return the money within 60 days. Be aware that if you're even one day late you may have to pay up to a 10% penalty. Be sure to verify the details before taking the money out of an IRA or 401K.

Stocks and Bonds:

If you own stocks and bonds, you can sell them to get cash to start your business.

Promissory Note Receivable:

If you have any notes receivable, you can sell these notes at a discount and get cash or you can borrow against them.

**II. Family and Friends**

Family and friends are another source of funding for a new business. More often than not, these are the people who know and trust your ideas and would consider supporting you with their personal finances. Many people utilize these resources, when starting their own businesses.

However, because of the personal relationships involved it can be much harder to borrow money from family and friends than from a bank. Those close to you might have a tendency to get over-involved in your business, giving feedback more often than you would like. Asking the right family members and friends is the key. You cannot discuss your business plans with everyone and you may not want to work with certain individuals in a business setting. Look for those people who have faith in you and your ideas and who you are comfortable working with. Make sure you have a concrete strategy plan and that they understand it and are on board with it.

Talk to them about your business so they feel comfortable with your idea and methodology. Give your business plan to them the same as you would do with a bank or any other lender. The key here is to cultivate their faith in you and your business. Clearly explain to them how you are planning to pay them back and stick to the payments as if you were working with a bank.

There are two ways, you can pay them back.

1.Plan a certain interest rate based on the days/months/years given to pay the money back. You can make the payment monthly or quarterly. Your payment could include interest only or principal and interest. If you are paying interest only, figure out when you will pay back the principal balance. When you give them a payment plan, stretch it over a longer period of time to pay them back. This way it will not put strain on your cash flow.

2.The second thing you can offer them is a small profit sharing plan. This means if your company makes a good profit, you will share that profit with them, depending on their investment. For example, if you borrow $100,000, every year you can give them 10% to 15% return on their investment with your profit. If you have five relatives and they each give you $100,000 then collectively you have $500,000 as a startup capital, or if you have 10 family or friends who invest $25,000 each then you will raise $250,000 as startup money.

If you are planning to raise money from your family and friends you need to know what kind of money they can offer.

One thing is certain, you must pay the money back. Doing so will build your reputation and character. Also, you never know if you will need to call them again in the future. Remember, every business has its ups and downs.

Prepare yourself for negative feedback. Not everyone will love your idea and not everyone will have the funds to give you. More often than not, a good idea is rejected a dozen times, before someone accepts it, faithfully.

### III.SBA Loan (Small Business Administration): www.sba.gov

SBA is a United States Government agency that is formed to provide support to small business owners and entrepreneurs. SBA provides guarantees to banks and commercial lenders, allowing them to lend money to small businesses. SBA does not give loans, It only guarantees the loan in the event that the loan goes into default. SBA covers the lender's loss and provides a guarantee of up to 80% of the loan.

**Some of the SBA loan programs,**

-SBA startup loan.

-SBA commercial loan

-SBA unsecured loan

-SBA minorities loan

-SBA women owned business grants

-SBA microloan

-SBA real estate loan

-SBA equipment loan

-SBA disaster loan

**SBA also has loans for the following**

-Working Capital

-Inventory And Supply

-Furniture and Fixtures

To find out more detail about these programs you can visit SBA website at www.sba.gov.

**IV. Government Loan And Grants:**

In addition to the SBA loan program there are other Federal State, local government business loans and grant programs.

**Here are few:**

USDA rural development loan www.usda.gov

This is loan program through United State Department of Agriculture; this is program specifically for rural areas. You can find out more about this program by visiting their website. There are several loans and grant programs for rural business initiatives, here are a few listed below that may be valuable to your business.

-Rural Community Development Initiative (RCDI)

-Rural Business Enterprise Grants (RBEG)

-Rural Business Opportunity Grants (RBOG)

-Rural Economic Development Loans (REDL)

-Rural Economic Development Grants (REDG)

-Rural Micro-Entrepreneur Assistance Program (RMAP)

An example of another possible business loan program, the REAP Renewable Energy for America Program shows the detail and breadth of possibilities. There is a vast range of topics that can be sought out with online research or using your local small business library or chamber of commerce. You can also check with your state. Most states have some type of small business assistance for loans and other kinds of help and counseling available. Your county and city may also have support for small business initiatives such as a grant loan, incubator or space to start a business at a reduced rent.

### V. Venture Capital (VC) or Angel Investor:

There are investors who invest in start-ups. They are called venture capitalists or angel investors. This is a high risk investment. When an angel investor sees long term growth potential, they make an investment for future profit. Venture Capitals do not lend money, they take equity and/or positions in the company. Venture capital is not limited to money. It can also include access to technical and managerial expertise. This is a very important source of funding for new starts-ups. Generally venture capitalists are wealthy investors, investment bankers, banks and other financial institutions.

### VI. Joint Venture (JV):

A joint venture is a business arrangement where two or more parties agree to pool their resources for the purpose of accomplishing a specific task. Each party is responsible for the cost, profit and loss. This could be a brand new business or an existing one. Pooling together funding reduces the risk of a new venture because the risk will be spread among the parties involved. A joint venture is a kind of general partnership. It is very important to have a joint venture agreement signed before starting a venture so that the terms and conditions are clear.

### VII. Private Lender:

There are some private lenders who can lend you money for your business. These lenders or private investors will lend you money, but a private lender invests for a high return. Their money could be expensive in the terms of interest rates and closing costs. There are private lenders such as [www.obeckcapita.com](http://www.obeckcapita.com), who lend out between $5000 to $25000 or who provide private loans for real estate. There are many other private individuals or companies who provide this type of loan. Private Lenders are also known as Hard Money Lenders.

### VIII. Private Investor/ Silent partners:

Private investors, also known as "silent partners," are looking for a high return. These silent partners can come in the form of an individual, or a company and will lend you the funds, but with terms and agreements. These agreements are frequently that they want profits sent to them every month.

Typically, they will give you the money upfront, as long as you run the business and share the profit with them. Most of the time, the private investor knows the entrepreneur. They may have had a business relationship in the past and are generally familiar with the entrepreneur's business reputation.

## IX. Partnership:

A partnership is when two or more people put their resources together and form a partnership to finance a business. Partnership contribution may be special knowledge, expertise or business connections. Sometimes a simple connection can bring a business to life.

*"Where there is a will there is always a way"*

# Chapter-7

# Location Machinery And Equipment

*"No one cheats you out of ultimate success, but yourself."*

-Ralph Waldo Emerson

**LOCATION:**

Location is of the utmost importance. One thing to take into consideration is what type of business you are starting. For example, if it is a retail business, then you need to be at the front of the road with more visibility, to attract attention. In contrast, if the company is related to manufacturing, you need a location where the power supply is adequate, skilled labor is available and machinery and equipment are highly accessible. If you are considering starting a hi-tech business, then you need to have highly- qualified, hi-tech labor available.

There are many aspects to take into consideration when thinking about location. Examples are: 1.) How much space will you need? 2.) What will the cost per sq. ft. or per month be? 3.) What location will be suitable for your new business?

In addition, you will also be paying for the utilities, maintenance (cleaning and repairs), taxes and insurance on the work space.

**1.Zoning Requirements:**

Make sure the building is zoned for the type of business you will be running. For example, industrial zoning, commercial zoning and retail zoning are three different kinds of zoning you might need to investigate for your particular type of business. Again, it is important to check the zoning requirements for the type of business you are planning to start.

**2.Safety:**

You have to make sure that the place of work is safe for you and your employees to work inside and outside the building and safe for clients and customers as well.

**3.Future Growth:**

Depending on the type of business you're starting, you may want to consider future growth in the location you're about to select. Is there any extra space you can rent if your business takes off?

**4.Size of Space:**

You need to do your homework to find out how much space you will need. In my experience, it takes less than you think. You want to first see if your business will grow. After all, leasing costs are an overhead cost and the lower overhead costs, better the cash flow.

**5. Renting Vs Buying:**

Again, depending on type of business you're going to start, most of the time you can lease (rent) the space. Exceptions include starting a franchise, such as McDonald's or Burger king or other specialized facilities. In that case, you may have to buy the land and the building. Most of the time however, you can lease the space.

**6. Taxes And Insurance:**

You need to the check property taxes and building insurance, most of the time the landlord will sign a triple net lease. That means you will have to pay a portion of the property tax and common area maintenance. Common area maintenance is also known as CAM. Be sure to check whether the liability and building insurance is included in CAM.

**7. Renovation:**

If your business requires a renovation or remodeling of the space you are about to lease, then find out who will pay for it before signing the lease. In most cases the cost of renovation can be negotiated in your lease. If you are signing a 3, 5, 7 or 10 years lease, the landlord can prorate the cost of renovation in your lease. That will save you money upfront which can be used for working capital or other expenses instead.

**8. Sign:**

Find out who will pay for your sign (if you need one). Find out what kind of sign is permitted in the area or in the building.

**9. IT-System, Power:**

The right internet connection and speed is vital for running the operations of your business, make sure your place of work supports the type of data connection you need to run your business competitively. Consider the cost of different internet connections and if you have to pay for it separately or if it can be included in your office space rent. Also look into, whether there is enough power supply to run your machinery and equipment.

**10. Janitorial Service and Trash Removal Service:**

Starting a business can create a lot of debris, find out if the landlord will provide trash removal services or if there is a common dumpster in the facility. Janitorial services will be needed for the office area, this may be included in your lease or you can hire a cleaning service independently.

**11. Exterior Maintenance:**

You need to know who will maintain the outside of the building, either you or the building owner will need to keep the exterior in working order making sure that the parking lot and the landscaping are professionally maintained. Expenses such as roofing, exterior painting or even snow removal need to also be considered.

### 12. Parking:

This goes without saying, but at the same time, it can often go forgotten. Be certain that there is enough parking for your potential employees and clients. It can be more than an inconvenience if clients struggle to park, every time they want to visit your business. This is the kind of aspect that can drive clients to competitors.

### 13. Demographics:

Your demographic is your target audience. When you are planning out your business, consider who your product or service will appeal to.

If you are planning to open a type of clothing store, for example, who will be wearing your clothes? Trendy men, in their 20's? Pregnant women? You will want to research this age demographic and be on the lookout for upcoming trends. Choose the location of your business with regards to the demographics of your customers and employees.

### 14. Foot Traffic:

In some businesses, foot traffic or walk-in traffic plays a very important role. You do not want to get struck in a corner of the building where no one can see you and potential customers have trouble locating you.

### Hiring a Realtor:

A good commercial leasing agent can help you find the right space. They are knowledgeable and can get you a good deal. They will work for you to negotiate the right deal. When you hire an agent make sure he or she is a commercial agent and has experience in leasing or sales. They have the necessary tools to check that all of your needs are met. Most of the time they are paid by the landlord, also a good real estate agent has knowledge of financing, zoning requirements and purchase/lease negotiations. When you are negotiating a purchase or lease, they will work for you to check on the zoning, power supply and other needs for your business.

**Machinery and Equipment:**

Now is the time to check what type of machinery and equipment you will need. You need to make a list of such items and find out the cost to buy versus leasing. It will be hard to get credit to purchase the machinery or equipment. Since you are starting out it will be better to lease. Leasing can save time and money. Leasing will give you a tax advantage because leasing or renting equipment and machinery is tax deductible. When you lease equipment you can return it after the lease is up or you can trade it in for bigger equipment or more technologically advanced equipment. A lot of time, the maintenance of the equipment is included in your lease.

**"Less debt, less danger"**

# Chapter-8

# Goal

*"When you change the way you look at things, the things you look at change"*

-Dr. Wayne Dyer

A goal is the anticipated result a person or a company plans and commits to reach. It is the anticipated result or development. A goal stops people from procrastinating and motivates them to start taking action.

**Commitment + Action= Reach a Goal**

**What are your goals?**

Write them down. It may take a few weeks to generate goals that are both attainable and well thought out.

Initially, do not worry too much about what you write down; the creative process is all about revision. In other words, you meet your goals. It may take some time, but if you are persistent with your goals, you will attain them.

Start with short-term goals, that are achievable. Seeing your goals written down will make them feel more real. In the beginning it is important to start with small, short term goals. Again, your goal must be in writing and you need to see it and review it periodically. So let's get started with your goal.

**For example:**

Let's say your goal in life is to be a successful businessman, or perhaps your goal is to be rich and famous. Maybe your goal is to start your business by January and generate X amount of revenue this year and so on.

You have a goal or an idea. Write it down and start working towards your goal. Your goal, your objective and your ambition are closely related. You can not have one without other.

**You can divide your goal:**

a. Short Term Goal

b. Long Term Goal

c. Life Time Goal

There are probably some thing you would like to achieve in weeks or months or ever in a year. Write them down.

Make sure your goals have purpose and a deadline. A goal is a plan with deadline.

**Here are few suggestions to help you start your goal.**

A. Start writing easy things to do that you like to complete.

B. Make a to-do list.

C. Set-up a realistic timeline to achieve your goal.

D. Organize your work place.

E. Organize your daily routine.

F. Reward yourself for achieving a goal.

G. Most importantly - get started.

**Short Term Goal:**

When setting a short term goal, give yourself enough time to complete it. Goal setting is planning. It is what you would like to achieve today, tomorrow, this week or this month. Write these goals down and start working towards them. You will be surprised to see how much easier progress is, just by breaking everything down into simpler steps.

**Long Term Goal:**

Long term goal are goals or plans you have for your business in the long term. What is the plan for your business in one, two, three, five years from now? In the beginning it will be hard to see five years from now but once you start your business and have some experience then you can assess where you would like to see your business in five years from now. You can go back to your long term goals and continue to revise them as you progress in your business.

Long term goals are something you would like to reach or achieve in years to come. Long term goals are an important way to see your self in the future. Long term goals make you think about how you hope to see yourself and your business in the coming years.

A smart business person knows the value of goal setting and achieving them. There was an article in INC., by Peter Vanden Bos.

*"Your company goals will only be effective if you have a clear vision of what you want to achieve and how"*

In an article, recently published, it was alluded to that more than 80% of 300 small business owners didn't keep track of their business goals and that 77% have yet to achieve their initial vision driving their company.

When writing a business goal it is better to do it as team. Get other integral employees involved and listen to their input, in working towards your goal. Remember, you cannot achieve a goal without your team working with you. Make sure to get input from your key employees and associates. Make it a matter of "OUR goal" rather than "MY goal". You will be surprised at how much easier it is to achieve your goal once you have your employees and associates on the same page as you.

**Your goal should include:**

Smart Goal

Specific

Measurable

Attainable

Relevant

Timely


A key facet in setting a goal is to avoid setting many goals in too short of a time period. As Rome was not build overnight, neither will your business. It will take time and hard work. There will be both successes and failures. Be patient and exercise discipline over your thoughts, especially when you have feelings of anxiety, over the outcome or the process of reaching a goal.

**Lifetime goal:**

"Lifetime Goals" are what you would like to achieve, in your lifetime. They can be broad and long-term. At this point, your lifetime goals may not be as important, but once you get your business up and running successfully, you need to set aside time to contemplate said goals. Of course this is only a suggestion and you can set up your lifetime goals at any time.

**Here are some examples of Lifetime Goals:**

A. Business Or Career Goals.

B. Financial Goals.

C. Family And Friends Goals.

D. Spiritual Goals.

E. Retirement Goals

F. Fitness Goals

G. Travel Goals

H. Public Service Or Volunteer Goals

*"Confidence comes naturally with success but, success comes only to those who are confident so, began your goal with great confidence"*

*-Melchor Lin.*

# Chapter-9

# Marketing And Sales

*"The aim of marketing is to know and understand the customer so well that the product or service fits him/her and sells it self"*

-Peter Drucker

**Marketing:**

Marketing refers to the process of translating and communicating the value of a good or service, to the customer, with the intention of selling the aforementioned. Marketing is a critical component of your business. 70% of the success of any business depends on a solid and well thought out strategy plan backed by an excellent product or service. The combination of a great product (or service) and a solid marketing plan can come close to guaranteeing success in your venture.

A solid marketing plan includes assessing the customer's need and their satisfaction. If you do not know how to market, your business your expertise alone will not be enough to get your business going. A good marketing plan helps to bring customers to your business. Gaining a customer's confidence and developing a trusting relationship helps sustain the future of your business via referrals and other potential avenue of revenue.

**Marketing Plan:**

Now is the time to develop a marketing plan. A marketing plan is a road map which outlines your company's overall marketing efforts. Your marketing plan should include your plan to target your customer. Here are some things that should be in your marketing plan:

**1. Introduction:**

Introduce your company to your customer and have your mission statement written up. Your company logo must be ready for use in advertising. If you are opening a new business introduce it as the "grand opening" or if you are in the buying business introduce it under "new management". No matter what kind of business you are about to start: from a restaurant, to a professional service, to a retail shop or to an internet based business, positioning your products or services begins with an introduction to your market.

**2. Describe Your Customer:**

Create a profile of your customer. Who will buy or use your product and services? It does not matter if you are selling business to business or business to customers. You need to understand your customers.

## 3. Your Marketing Objective:

What are your goals and objectives? What would you like to achieve with your marketing efforts?

What will be your ROI (return on investment)? For example, if you are spending X amount of $ what kind of return are you expecting? if you spend $1000, what kind of return will you get?

**ROI=REVENUE/MONEY SPEND**

## 4. Budget:

How much money are you planning to spend on marketing? Create your weekly, monthly and even annual budget. Budgeting is important, as it will give you a clear lens into how much money you need for marketing. You can use a percentage of the profits to come up with your marketing budget.

## 5. Marketing Medium:

Where will your marketing dollar go? Possible avenues include print advertising, direct mail, local newspaper, the internet, social media, radio, TV and so on.

## 6. Track Your Marketing:

It is very important for you to track where your customers are coming from. Which type of advertising is bringing you the most customers and which type of advertising is not bringing you any customers. This will save lot of money in the long run. If you are not getting any customers from a particular advertisement, you need to drop that advertisement and try a different form of marketing or advertising.

## 7. Test Your Marketing:

In your marketing plan you must have a system to test particular marketing or advertising strategies before spending lots of money. Testing your marketing is a must. It does not matter how solid your marketing plan may seem to be, you must test it before committing to a large advertising campaign.

### Marketing has three functions:

A. Advertising and promotion

B. Sales

C. Packaging and delivering


### A. Advertising and promotion.

Advertising is a form of communication for marketing a product to encourage or persuade the public to take a look at your products and services.

**Types of Advertising:**

1. Direct mail

2. Print advertising

3. Online advertising

4. Social media

5. Radio and TV advertising

6. Verbal (word of mouth)

7. E-mail marketing

8. Billboards

9. Cell phone advertising

**1. Direct mail:**

Mailing postcards, flyers or letters directly to the customer is an example of direct mail. For the best and most effective postcard mailers, get your postcards printed in bulk and mail them out to your target market periodically. The USPS has a program called "Every Door Direct mail." Here you can mail postcards at about .17 cents per postcard plus you can print them at about 0.3-0.5 cents per postcard. For more information, check out www.USPS.com.

## 2. Printed Advertising:

Running advertisements in newspapers, magazines and/or giving out flyers and brochures to people or businesses.

## 3. Online Advertising:

Advertising online is a great way to build awareness and traffic to your business. Sites such as Google, Youtube and Facebook allow you to create advertisements and even arrange it so that they are more prevalent among geographically relevant areas.

## 4. Social Media Advertising:

Advertising on social media can take place on websites, such as Facebook, LinkedIn and Google+, but can also take place on apps. such as Instagram. Do your research and discover which mediums would be best for you and your business.

Let's say for example, that you do not want to advertise directly, online. You can create a business profile, on LinkedIn. This way, potential employees and customers will see your page and want to know more about what you do. Social media allows you to promote your products and services for free, while also engaging with your audience

## 5. Radio and TV advertisements:

Depending on the type of business you are starting and how much money you are planning to spend, you can advertise on the radio and TV. Just remember, this can be expensive for a start-up.

### 6. Verbal (Word of mouth):

One of the best ways to advertise is by word of mouth (verbal). This will be free advertisement. In order to do word of mouth advertisement, you must have a unique product or outstanding customer service/care. Customers feel compelled to let other people know about your business.

### 7. Email marketing:

Set-up a system and have people sign up for e-mail. Once you have your database ready, start sending out a weekly promotion, or a newsletter announcement for incentives, such as sales or free gifts.

If your database has even 50 people, start sending out emails and work on adding more individuals, to your database. For example, if you add 5 peoples to your database every day, you can get 1500 contacts in your e-mail database within year. This method, for gaining customers, is highly cost-effective.

### 8. Billboards:

Again, depending on the type of business and how big a budget you have, you can advertise on outdoor or indoor billboard signs. This can get expensive, especially if you are just starting out.

### 9. Cell phone advertising:

This is a new way of advertising. You can send text messages to cell phones or send advertisements to smart phones. You can create a database of people to send text messages or advertisements via phone.

We have gone over some of the advertising strategies you can use as you are starting up your business. You can pursue different marketing techniques as your business gets going. Some of the advertising strategies described here are free or of very nominal cost. Check out the options and see which one works best for your type of business.

There are 2 types of advertisements:

**A. Lead generating, Direct response Advertising or** aggressive advertising:

All of your advertising focuses on getting the phone to ring, having a customer walk in or having a customer logon online. This will start generating revenue for you immediately. For a start-up business this is the best kind of advertising.

**B. Name Recognition or Passive Advertising:**

This will get your name out, but to a very few customers initially. This is long term advertising strategy. You need to have deep pockets for this kind of advertising. It takes years to build a brand and to attract customers to your business. As a new start-up this will not be the best way to market your business.

**Promotions:**

Promotions are short term incentives to attract customers. They run for a limited time. For example, coupons are promotions. *"Buy one get one free"* is an example of a promotion. Giving out drinks or other items for free is a promotion. Promotions involve short term strategies to move the product, whereas advertising is a long term strategy to build a customer base and a brand.

**Comparison Chart:**

| Item | Advertising | Promotion |
|---|---|---|
| Time | Long term | Short term |
| Price | Expensive | Not very expensive |
| Sales | Lead to sale | Directly related to sale |
| Example | Doing advertisement | Giving free coupons, gift, t-shirt, drink, toys and novelties |
| Result | Slowly | Immediate |

*"Marketing is not the art of finding clever ways to dispose off what you make. It is the art of creating genuine customer value"*

-Philip Kotler

**Sales:**

Sales, refers to the act of selling products or services in exchange for money or other compensation. Sales is the generation of your income. Thus far, we have discussed how to spend money to create revenue.

Just remember, everyone is a salesperson. We have all been selling our skills and ideas in one form or another, for years. Examples of this can be seen in sending applications to college, selling your resume and capabilities to potential employers, etc.

Now it is the time to come up with a realistic sales projection for your business.

**What is a sales projection?**

A sales projection is the amount of revenue a company expects to have in the future, it is a sales forecast.

There are a number of software programs available for sales forecasting. You can start with a 12 months projection. This will give you an idea of how much revenue you will generate in the next 12 months. You can always revise your forecast. If you do not have forecasting software, you can always use a 12 month column pad or template.

**Sales team:**

Every company needs a good sales team to make sales. They need good sales people to help the company grow. Without a good sales team, your company will not prosper. You can spend as much as you like on advertising and promotion but if you do not have a strong sales force, you risk great failure. Unless you already have an experience in sales, consider getting sales training. There are hundreds maybe thousands, of books, tapes, websites, webinars and seminars available to improve your and your employee's sales skills. Selling is an art you need to master and enjoy. As I said before, the sales team will put your company on the map. **Below are ten quotes from one the greatest salesman Mr. Zig Zigler to encourage you.**

1. "If you dream it you can achieve it"

2. "Your attitude, not your aptitude will determine your altitude"

3. "A goal properly set is halfway reached"

4. "If you go looking for a friend, you are going to find they are scarce and if you go out to be a friend you will find them everywhere"

5. "Expect the best. Prepare for the worst. Capitalize on what comes. "

6. "People don't buy for logical reasons. They buy for emotional reasons."

7. "There has never been a statue erected to honor a critic."

8. "People often say motivation doesn't last. Neither does bathing—that's why we recommend it daily."

9. "You will get all you want in life, if you help enough other people get what they want."

10. "Remember that failure is an event, not a person."

**Packaging and delivery**

**Packaging:**

The third item for marketing is packaging and delivering your product and services to your customers. Packaging contains identity, description, protection of the products and promotions, keep it clean and neat looking. Your packaging affects everything from the display of your product in the store to the display of the product when it reaches in your customer's hand. Attractive packaging will help selling your product. Packaging is an important part of marketing a product. It catches the customer's attention and at the same time provides information about your products to your customer/s. Thirdly, it protects the product from damage.

**Delivery:**

Delivering product to your customer is also part of marketing. If delivering the products to the person you need to present the products in a bag, make sure your business logo/ contact information is easily visible and accessible. If delivering to an inbox, make sure information about your company is readily accessible as well. Even in a service business you can give out your receipt with your company information/logo on it or include a promotion or a coupon with your receipt.

Packaging and delivery must have marketing in mind so that the customer can make a repeat purchase.

*"Marketing takes day to learn, unfortunately takes a lifetime to master"*

*-Philip Koter*

# Chapter-10

# Management

*"Good management is the art of making problems so interesting and their solution so constructive that everyone wants to get to work and deal with them"*

-Paul Hawken

**Managing Your Business**

Management is typically identified as the act of controlling, facilitating and making decisions in regards to a team or business. A good leader creates an effective management team and grants them the authority and responsibility to complete the tasks at hand. The management team has the responsibility of getting the job done accurately, effectively and on time.

**Manager:** Managers get the job done. A good manager is both a student and a teacher. Managers have to have strong leadership qualities to lead in any business.

**Leader:** Peter Drucker states that *management* is doing things right and *leadership* is doing the right things. Leaders make things happen by their positive influence.

Managers and leaders both need to have a strong presence to make the business grow and prosper.

**1. Motivate:** You need to have fantastic motivational skills. This will help to encourage yourself, as well as the people you work with.

**2. Set Goals:** Set goals with your team. Working towards a unified ambition builds community and helps all of the gears move more efficiently.

**3. Delegate:** After setting goals, delegate responsibilities to members of your team. Breaking up the work allows people to focus in on specific tasks.

**6. Treat Everyone Equally:** Treat associates and employees both equally and fairly.

**7. Be A Good Listener:** Listening is an art form that everyone can improve upon.

**9. Empathy:** Empathy is the ability to understand and share the feelings of others. Empathy and listening go hand-in-hand.

**10. Persuasion Skills:** Persuasion is a great skill to have in the workplace. Whether you are presenting a new product to a client or your boss, persuasion will help you convey your point directly.

**11. Focus:** The key to success as a manager or leader is focus. Focus on your goal, your job and your business. You will definitely succeed. Just as people say, "Do not take your eyes off the ball."

**12. Hiring the Right Person:** Hire the right person for the job, someone who understands your goal and can do good job (in some cases even better than you).

**14. Avoid Waste:** Use cost-cutting methodology, whenever possible (without compromising quality.) Train others and promote a culture of zero waste tolerance.

**15. Finances:** Understand the value of money. This is one of your primary goals as a business owner. The goal of a manager is to create profit. A company must have profits to stay in business.

**Managing your Business**

When you are starting a business you are going to wear many hats, until you have the revenue to hire other people. The good news is that you will do great. Have confidence in your ability to get the job done. After all, you started the business and you are the boss. You are also the employee, the bookkeeper, the manager, the leader, the salesman and the technician. You will gain a great deal of confidence and valuable experience as you assume so many roles and wear so many different hats. Whatever needs to be done you will do it yourself or you will get it done by someone else.

*"Either run the day or the day runs you"*

-Jim Rohn

**Systemize:**

Systemize your business; this will help you run your business smoothly. Setting up a system is very important for your business. As a manager you should try to set-up a system for everything. It may take you a bit of time, but it will be well worth it.

## What is a System?

A system is a process which everyone follows to do the same job exactly the same way to attain the same result. When setting up a system think about the iconic McDonalds and the system that they utilize. It does not matter which McDonald's you go to, you will get the same Big Mac product every time. So think, plan and set up a good system. A good system is step by step process from start to finish.

Systemize your business; this will help you run your business efficiently. Writing out a model of what you want and how you want to execute it is of the utmost importance.

### Here are few systems you will need:

**1. Marketing System:**

Set up a system to get new business, get customers and generate leads.

**2. Sales System:**

You need a system to convert these customers into clients and to convert the leads into sales.

**3. Production System:**

Set up a system for producing a product with same quality every time.

### 4. Service System:

Set up a system where the customer can experience the same great services every time.

### 5. Accounting System:

Set up a system for accounts and bookkeeping either manually or with a computer.

### 6. Hiring And Training System:

Set up a system for your hiring process, in order to filter out great potential employees for your business. Similarly set up a training system to train both old (refresher) and new employees.

### 7. Delivery System:

Set up step by step procedure, to deliver your product to your customers.

### 8. Follow up System:

Set up a system to follow up with your customer. Create a database of your entire clientele, so that you can keep track of your clients and they will repeat business with you, or even send you referrals.

Until a business activity is systematized, it will always depend on a few employees who know how to do the job correctly. Once it is systematized, it can be duplicated by any ordinary employee.

A system is set up by the trial and error method. It will take some time, but once it is set up it will double or triple your efforts and increase your efficiency. Consider reading an instructional book by Brian Tracy titled, "Now Build A Great Business" for further information.

*"Managers today have to do more with less and get better results from limited resources more than ever before"*

*-Brian Tracy*

# Chapter-11

# Accounting

*"That which we persist in doing becomes easier, not that the task itself has become easier but our ability to perform it has improved"*

*-Ralph Waldo Emerson*

Accounting is a system of recording, reporting, analyzing and summarizing the financial transactions of a business. A person who does such a work is known as an Accountant.

Bookkeeping is a process of accounting. In bookkeeping, a record of financial transactions is kept on a day to day basis. A person who does this work is known as a bookkeeper. Both accountants and bookkeepers keep all financial transactions and records very accurate, up to date and comprehendible. Bookkeeping is a vital part of the accounting process. An accountant prepares reports based on the information accumulated by the bookkeeping process. Examples of such reports include financial statements, tax returns, financial reports and profit and loss statements. Calculating profit is a critical part of the accounting process. Likewise, in accounting, one must know how to measure income and expenses to determine profits and losses.

You can certainly understand the importance of accounting and bookkeeping. It is one of the first things you need to set up for your business. The importance of having a very good accounting system can not be overemphasized. There may be a day when you need to know the income and expenses, money coming in and money going out. There is very cost effective software available which can do the job. As a business owner you need to know how you are doing financially every day. How much money do you have in the bank? Which bills are due this week, next week, this month or next month?

**ACCOUNTING SYSTEMS:**

A good accounting and bookkeeping system is the cornerstone of any successful company. It does not matter if you are a mom and pop shop, a one person business or a giant corporation with numerous employees. In the very beginning when you are just starting to plan your business, before you spend any money on your business, you need to set up an accounting system so you can record your startup costs.

**Here are some tips to help you get started:**

1.**Record keeping system:** keep all the financial documents, employee records, invoices, purchase orders, bills, receipts, bank statements, tax, corporate papers, LLC papers, loan papers and other business records organized.

2.**Filing System:** Set up a good filing system for invoices, purchase orders, bills, accounts receivable, account payable. Make sure to file all important financial records, contracts, employee files and tax returns. The best way to do so is to first label a folder. An alphabetical filing system uses either company name or the last name of the person in alphabetical order to organize and systemize the filing process. Start putting all necessary documents into the file folder. There are two ways to file a document in the folder, the most recent document can be filed in front of file folder or in back of the file folder. In either case, you should always file same way. When you hire a bookkeeper let him or her know if you file forward or backward, he/she will know where to look for a document, consistency will make everything easy to find. Now a days there are a number of software programs for digital filing. If you are computer savvy you may want to set up a digital filing system. Again the concept is the same: organizing documents into easy to use files. The difference is that one is a hard paper copy and the other is paperless.

**3. Tax payment system:** A system to file taxes with the IRS, state, local and other tax authorities. Your payroll taxes need to be filed with the IRS and state taxes need to be filed with the state (if there is one) city taxes need to be filed with the city (if your city collects taxes). Keep records of everything you file. Your social security and medical taxes also need to be filed with the IRS. Your sale taxes needs to be filed with the state or the city.

**4. Accounts Receivable System:** You need to set up a system to collect and deposit all of your income checks. You do not want to hold the check for three or four days before depositing it into the bank. It is best to deposit the check in your account right away because it may take ten days for the check to clear from the bank.

**5. Account Payable System:** You need to set up a system to pay bills, You should schedule payments for your bills. When you receive a bill, put a payment date on the bill. Some bills will need to be paid every month, such as phone bills, electric bills and charge card bills- these can be set up to be paid automatically online. Other bills, such as a vendor's bill can be paid in thirty, sixty or ninety days, depending on how much time you can get from your vendor. Most of the big corporations pay their bills in sixty to ninety days, this allows them to collect their money before paying you.

*"Collect early pay late, buy low sell high"*

**6. Payroll System:** Set up a date for your payroll. This can be either bi-weekly or monthly. In addition, set up a day of week your employees will be paid. For example, if you are paying weekly you can set up your employee's paychecks to be distributed on Friday for the previous week. Most companies hold one paycheck to establish the payday. Once the pay day has been established, you need to determine if you are paying on an hourly basis or by salary. If you are paying hourly, every employee needs to have a time card and time clock to record the number of hours worked by punching-in when arriving and punching-out when leaving for the day.

You, your bookkeeper or your manager will collect all the time sheets and calculate the hours worked. Now a days there are electronic clock systems you can use for your employees to sign in and out. This system will automatically calculate the number of hours worked and send the information directly to the bookkeeper for payroll. A salaried employee will get a fixed salary, which is easier to calculate and prepare a payroll for.

**7. Data Entry System:** Have a system to post all data, such as sales, sales receipts, invoices, purchase orders and all other important financial data. Based on the type of business you are in, the data may need to be posted daily. Some data may be posted weekly. It depends on the importance and urgency of the data. For example, if you post all payable invoice data once a week, it should work just fine. You will have time to set up a payment schedule for those bills.

**8. Purchasing System:** Depending on the size and type of business you are starting, you will need some type of system to purchase supplies, raw materials, tools etc. You need to be frugal with purchases. It does not matter who is buying! whether it is yourself, your bookkeeper or your purchasing agent. Be sure everyone purchases items on sale. Also look to buy with credit instead of cash. Many companies will set up a credit account for you. If you shop around and do your research, you can get better supplies at a better price. For example, ink toner can be less expensive. If you buy it on sale or buy from a supplier who offers a discount or a sale price, you can save lot of money on an annual basis.

**9. System for Reports:** You need to see your financial report on a monthly or quarterly basis. A long time ago we use to get a report of profits and losses on a quarterly basis. Nowadays, if your system is computerized you can get a financial report every day, every week or every month. All of these different types of reports will help guide your business in the right direction.

**10. System for Renewal of License:** When you start a business, over time, you will need to renew your license. Business entities, such as a corporation or LLC require professional license renewals. These are very basic licenses that need to be renewed every year. Depending on the type of business you are in, you may need many different licenses, which need to be renewed periodically. It is important to have a system in place to renew them when they become due. Accounting is the department to keep track of all your renewals. Let your accounting department handle this task.

**11. Budgeting System:** Your accounting department is responsible for the budget. They can prepare the budget with the help of other employees and good record-keeping practices. The budget may be prepared monthly, quarterly or annually.

## ACCOUNTING METHOD

**There are two types of accounting methods:**

a. Cash Basis: This method means you record income when received and expenses when they are paid. This method is used by most all small business, because it is simple.

b.Accrued Method: This method means recording the income when it is earned, not when you get paid and recording expenses when they are incurred, not when you pay them.

To figure out which method suits your business needs, confirm with your accountant who will be able to help you to set-up the best accounting method for your business.

## When to hire a Bookkeeper?

You must plan before hiring a bookkeeper. First do you have enough money to pay a bookkeeper? Second, do you have enough work for a book keeper? Also consider doing it yourself either manually or with bookkeeping software. Other options include outsourcing your bookkeeping until you need a full time bookkeeper. There are many individuals and small bookkeeping companies around town who will charge by the hour or on a fixed rate basis to do your bookkeeping. Another option is to hire a secretary/bookkeeper who can do both jobs.

## When do you need a CPA or accountant?

Whether you handle your own accounting or someone else in your company does, to start you need a good CPA who can guide you to set things up your accounting system properly. You also need an accountant to help you understand different tax advantages and deductions. Once the system is set up, you can use an accountant once a month for filing reports or once a year for preparing your taxes. Again, you need to assess how much work is to be done, how much money you will need to pay the accountant and if you can do this yourself.

**The Bottom line:** You need to have a good accounting system to keep track of the income and expenses. If you like to do things manually, you can get a ledger or column pad from your office store. Alternatively, you can buy software to keep a solid record of all your receipts, expenses, income and other important documents.

**Bank Account:** It is very important to have a business bank account separate from your personal bank account. Likewise, keep personal and business income and expenses separate. It is not a good idea to co-mingle funds. Even if you are operating as proprietor for your business, it is better to pay for business expenses by check or by business charge card, not in cash.

**Petty Cash Account:** Petty cash is a cash account used for small business expenses/purchases or to reimburse employees for small expenses. Petty cash must be accounted for and safeguarded from theft. Petty cash must be written down as money in and money out. Audit your petty cash once a month for accuracy. Petty cash starts around $50 to $100. Once the petty cash amount goes down, you can replenish it to the same amount. An example of petty cash: an employee purchases something for $10 (donuts for a meeting) and needs to be reimbursed.

*"The common questions that get asked in business, why? That is a good question but an equally valid question is why not"*

*-Jeffrey Bezos*

# Chapter-12

# Budgeting And Forecasting

*"Nothing can stop the man with right mental attitude from achieving his goal"*

-Thomas Jefferson

This chapter deals with the Budgeting and Forecasting of your business.

**What is Budgeting?**

Budgeting is planning and allocating funds for distribution among different activities in business. When you start a business or if you are already in business, you need to have a budget for different types of expenses. Budgeting will give you an idea of how much you can spend on certain items for example, advertising, raw materials, machinery & equipment and monthly supplies. Some expenses are fixed like rent or mortgage payments, machinery and equipment payments and car or truck payments. Others are variable, such as supplies, raw materials, marketing and advertising. These expenses changes every month and are known as variable expenses. Budgeting will give you an idea of what to expect for your expenses so you will not be surprised when the bill arrives.

Budgeting is a very good management tool. It also set forth a plan of action to achieve your financial goals, measure your company performance and helps you avoid adverse financial situations that may arrive.

**7 Reasons why budgeting is necessary;**

1. Allows you to have some idea about the money you need to run your business.

2. It will help you to be frugal with your money.

3. Budgeting will help you to achieve your goal much faster.

4. Budgeting will limit how much money you will spend on certain projects or operations.

5. Budgeting is your financial road map.

6. Budgeting will help you with your plan for future growth.

7. Budgeting can be used as a tracking tool.

**How To Budget?**

There are a number of software programs available to you. You can do your budgeting with software or you can do it manually by using a spreadsheet. You can have one budget for the whole company or you can break it down for different operations or departments.

For example, you can have a budget for accounting, a budget for marketing, a budget for payroll and a budget for purchasing. When you are doing budgeting, be as realistic as possible, use past data to come up with your budget. If you do not have any past data, use industry standards to come up with your budget plan. Outline the expected income and expenses based on actual data or industry standards.

## Sample Budgeting Template:

| NET INCOME | JAN | | FEB | | MARCH | |
|---|---|---|---|---|---|---|
| | Budget | Actual | Budget | Actual | Budget | Actual |
| Income 1 | | | | | | |
| Income 2 | | | | | | |
| Total: | | | | | | |
| EXPENSES | | | | | | |
| Officers Salary | | | | | | |
| Employee Payroll | | | | | | |
| Payroll Tax | | | | | | |
| Out side Labor | | | | | | |
| Rent | | | | | | |
| Office Supply | | | | | | |
| RAW MATERIAL | | | | | | |
| Insurance | | | | | | |
| Postage/delivery | | | | | | |
| Utilities | | | | | | |
| Phone/Internet | | | | | | |
| Advertising | | | | | | |
| Travel | | | | | | |
| Training | | | | | | |
| TOTAL | | | | | | |

## What is Forecasting?

Forecasting is the process of making future trends (based on current/past data) which has not yet been observed.

For business, forecasting is used to create a budget. In other words, forecasting is a part of budgeting. Forecasting comes from experience, knowledge of your product, knowledge of business and to some degree intuition. When initially starting your business, forecasting will not be very important; however, budgeting will help you tremendously.

*"You may never know what results come from your action, but if you do nothing there will be no result"*

*-Mahatma Gandhi*

# Chapter-13

# Inventory

*"The mind is everything. what you think you become"*

*-Buddha*

**Inventory**

Raw materials, unfinished items, finished goods, merchandise on hand; these are all considered to be inventory. Inventory is a business asset that is ready or will be ready for sale.

Be conscious of your inventory. Merchandise, finished goods and raw materials that are just sitting there will cost you money. Try and focus on keeping a low inventory. Inventory takes up space, as a high storage cost, may require insurance and the initial investment may incur interest adding to the overall costs of your business. If you do have a large inventory, you can eliminate much of it by using sales, promotions, exchanges and giveaways to keep your inventory moving.

**Inventory Management:**

**1. Low Inventory:**

Using historic data or experience, project how much supply you will need and when you will need it. This is based on your inventory on that date.

**2. Control System:**

Use electronic interchange (EDI) or barcode scanning to help you control your inventory accurately.

**3. An Inventory List:**

It is important to have an inventory list to know what items you have. It will help you dispose off old items and get fresh or new ones if necessary. A key point in inventory management is, knowing what you have in hand and how to move it. It is a process of moving goods out and getting goods in! keep your inventory constantly moving. Immaculate record keeping is the key to maximizing your inventory's value.

**4. Inventory Tax:**

Keep a good record of your inventory for tax purposes. You may have to pay taxes on some types of inventory.

**5. Management Software:**

Depending on what type of business you are in and how much inventory you have? You may consider investing in inventory management software. There are many types of inventory softwares which are completely automated. You can track your inventory by the click of the mouse.

## 6. Avoid Theft Of Inventory:

Theft is an unfortunate part of the business and is something that you should take into consideration. Many businesses lose money and goods to theft every year. Make sure your staff knows how to keep track of inventory with a secure inventory management system. Only you or a very trusted employee should review or edit your inventory management data or run your inventory management software.

## 7. Visual Inspection Of Inventory:

Check your inventory by visual inspection. You can get a good idea if something is missing or if you have a low or high stock of certain goods by conducting a manual count of inventory called physical inventory.

## 8. Supplier On Board:

Have your supplier on board with you. We call this supplier managed inventory. They can be notified as soon as an item is sold. This can be done by giving your supplier access to inventory data which they can use for sales reports and future planning.

## 9. Delivery To Customer:

Have a system to deliver your product to your customers as soon as they order it. This will cut down on your inventory turn-around time. This is the time from order placement to delivery.

### 10. Product Turnaround time:

Have a system to track which products move fast and which products take more time to move. That way you will know which items you should invest into more and which items you might want to offer at discount.

### 11. Borrow Money On Inventory:

If you have a large inventory or the economy has slowed down and you have a lot of goods sitting on the shelves, you can borrow against your inventory to get some of your money back until the inventory starts moving again and is sold. This will help your cash flow.

*"Planning is bringing the future into present so that you can do something about it now"*

-Alan Lakein.

# Chapter-14

# Insurance

*"In this business by the time you realize you are in trouble it is too late to save your self unless you are running scared all the time, you are gone"*

-Bill Gates

Insurance is a way of minimizing your risk. When you buy insurance you transfer risk to the insurance company. When you are in business you will invariably have some liabilities. Your risk depends on what type of business you are starting. Some businesses have higher risks than others. For example, if you are running a manufacturing business, your risk is higher than someone running an online internet business. You and your business are at risk for any mishaps that could result in loss of money or even a potential lawsuit. Some examples of possible insurance risks include: someone tripping and falling on your property, the possibility of office equipment getting stolen, the product you are manufacturing causes injuries or your office may burn down or get damaged in a natural disaster.

These things may/may not happen, but if they did then that kind of risk is minimized by insurance. Think about the insurance needed for your business, but do not get over-insured because your finances may be limited. When starting out, take a suitable basic insurance policy. In any case, insurance is a must.

**Type of insurance a small business owner needs.**

**1. General Liability Insurance:** This policy will cover both defense and damages to you. This type of policy is useful incase an employee, customer, product, or service causes or allegedly causes injury or damage to a third party.

**2. Property Insurance:** This insurance is important if you own a building. Even if you don't own a building, if you have a business, personal property such as office equipment, computers, machinery and other business equipment are protected. This policy will protect you from fire, theft, natural disasters, riots, vandalization etc.

**3. Commercial Auto Insurance:** This policy will cover your work vehicles: cars, SUV's, Vans, Trucks, as well as the products and equipment within those vehicles from damage and collision.

**4. Workers Compensation:** This type of insurance provides medical benefits for employees who get injured on the job. It provides them loss of pay. As a business owner, if you decide to hire an employee, it's a good idea to have this policy in place.

**5. Professional Liability Insurance or Error and Omission (E&O):** This type of insurance covers damages for failure to or improperly providing professional services. It is applicable for any professional firm such as law firms, accounting firms or consulting firms. It is also applicable for notaries, real estate agents, insurance agents, mortgage loan officers, hair salons and technology service providers to name a few..

**6. Data Breach Insurance:** This insurance covers data breaches, either electronically or in a paper form, such as stolen credit cards, loss of personal information and other forms of stolen data

**7. Officers And Directors Insurance:** This insurance covers the company officers and directors. Their actions may affect the profitability and or operations of the business. This type of insurance provides legal protection from these actions.

**8. Owners Policy (BOP):** This is an umbrella policy. It provides protection for property insurance, vehicle insurance, liability insurance and business interruptions etc.

**9. Product Liability Insurance:** If you are manufacturing a product that could cause harm, this insurance will cover the liability for the product.

**10. Business Income insurance:** This insurance provides disability coverage for your business. This insurance will pay money if the business temporarily shuts down or if a personal disability limits your ability to carry on the business.

**11. Health Insurance:** This insurance will cover you, your family, your employees and their families. Be aware, there are lots of changes taking place in health insurance policies.

Your insurance needs will depend on the type of business you are in. Whether you are starting a business or buying a business, there are many variables that determine the right insurance for your business including your business activity, location, whether or not you have any employees and so on. The best course of action will be (a) check your budget (b) check with your CPA and (c) check with insurance agents. When starting a business you have limited cash, so you can get an insurance policy which is basic. Later on you can add more insurance as needed.

*"In order to succeed, your desire should be greater than your fear of failure"*

*-Bill Casby.*

# Chapter-15

# Hiring

*"The only way to do great work is to love what you do, if you have not found it yet, keep looking do not settle."*

-Steve Jobs

Once your business is booming you cannot keep up with work, you keep falling behind. This is when you should think about hiring employees. Consider how many hours of work you have, then decide if you need a full time employee or a part time employee. Another thing to consider is whether you can outsource or subcontract your work. Outsourcing is a way to hire someone on a freelance basis for a specific task. The advantage of outsourcing is that you do not have the traditional employer/ employee obligations.

Think about your long term goals for growth. Where would you like to be? Do you like to manage people? Do you prefer to stay small? As you know managing other people can be challenging at times, yet rewarding. Employees in addition to bringing talent and energy to your business, also bring challenges: they require benefits, they might get sick, they will have family situations, they must be given vacations, holiday pay and health insurance. All of these factors will come in to play once you are ready to hire someone. Having an employee who can help you generate more revenue is definitely very positive for your business. You need employees to grow your business to the next level. Sometimes employees do a better job than you. If you have an employee you can delegate your work too and then you get more time to focus on growing business. They will bring a different energy to your company. When you hire an employee not only you are helping your company get more work done or helping a person make a living, but also you are helping society as a whole. You are creating a productive citizen and helping the larger economy grow as well.

**Before you hire an employee you need to prepare the following:**

**1. Set up a payroll system**: This can be done either with computer software or manually. There are many software programs available for payroll. Some are free and others cost money. Good software will automatically prepare paychecks with proper withholdings.

**2. Get an employer identification number (EIN):** You may already have this when you set up your company. If not, you need to get an EIN from the IRS. This is your tax id number. It will work like a SSN (social security number) for your business.

**3. Set up Record keeping for withholding tax:** You need to keep records of employment taxes for four years, so it's best to have a good record keeping system in place. There are three types of withholding taxes.

**a.FEDERAL INCOME TAX WITHHOLDING:** Every employee must sign an IRS form W-4 withholding exemption certificate on or before date of employment. This form is then sent to the IRS.

**b.FEDERAL WAGE AND TAX STATEMENT:** Every year the employer issues a W2 (wage and tax statement) to his/her employee to report all the income and withholding taxes he or she paid from Jan. 1st to Dec. 31st of that year. Each year the employer must report wages paid and taxes withheld to the IRS. Employees must get a copy of their W2 by Jan 31st for the previous year for their taxes. Employers must send a copy of the W2 to Social Security Administration by the last day of Feb.

**c.STATE TAXES:** If your state has income taxes, then you need to have state withholding income taxes. You must consult with your CPA to set up withholdings properly.

**4.Workers Compensation Insurance:** All businesses with employees need to provide workers compensation insurance coverage. You need to talk to your insurance agent about the coverage or check with your state's regulations.

**5.Verification System:** Before you hire an employee you need to set up a system for background checks, validity of references and work eligibility in USA. Federal law requires employees to verify an employee's eligibility to work in United States with in 3 days of hiring. Employees must complete form I-9 for employee eligibility verification. These documents must be kept for 3 years.

**Background checks** generally cost 20-30 dollars per employee. There are many companies that can provide this type of verification. You must get written permission from your prospective employee to do a background check.

**References:** Before you hire an employee you need to check their references. Check with their previous employer for work history verification, job performance etc.

**6.Employment Application and Testing:** Along with a resume you need to have all prospective employees fill out an application for employment and an authorization for a background check. You can find employment applications in office supply stores and online.

**Testing:** Depending on the type of work your prospective employee will be doing, it may be helpful to have a system to test their knowledge. A simple test can be done about what they know. You can also conduct a personality test to see if their personality would be a good fit for your company. The good news is you can find these tests online and put them to use in your system.

When you are very small company or startup, you have to do all of these things by yourself, but when you start to grow you can have someone in your office to do these tests and verifications for the company.

**7.Notice:** You are required to have certain posters in the workplace for employees about their rights and for employers about their responsibilities under Labor Laws. Also, there should be posters outlining employee's safety that are easily visible. You can get these posters online from the Labor Department.

**8. Interview Process:** It is best to have a two step interview process.

1. For part one, have your prospective employee complete an application, sign the authorization for background check, and get their references verified. Review all materials presented by the applicant. Give all the information to the interviewer who will be conducting the interviews.

2. Next, set up an appointment for face to face interviews:

-Review each candidates application package.

-Set interviews 20 minutes apart.

-Give the same amount of time to each prospective employee.

-Supply the interviewee with information they may need to prepare for the interview.

-Prepare your interview questions in advance.

-Make sure the interviewee feels comfortable.

-Control the meeting.

-Ask pointed & relevant questions.

-Talk about your company, your vision and mission.

-Listen carefully to both what they are saying and how they are saying it.

-Observe their body language.

-Discuss about salary and compensation.

-Find out what they looking for? and offer a competitive salary with benefits.

-Keep the time short and sweet.

-Remember you want the best candidate for the job, so sell your company and your offer.

**Record Keeping:**

Keep all employee records confidential and secure. You need to keep these records for a long time. Some states have laws to keep records for a set number of years. You need to verify the laws in your state.

*"Leadership is art of getting someone else to do something you want done because you want to do it."*

*-Dwight D. Eisenhower.*

# Chapter-16

# Policy And Procedure

*"You can not over estimate the need to plan and prepare. In most of the mistakes I have made there has been this common thing of inadequate planning beforehand. You really cannot over prepare in business"*

-Chris Corrigan

## POLICY

### What is a policy?

Policies are guidelines, rules and principles set by a company for everyone in the organization to follow, in order to achieve both short term and long term goals.

## PROCEDURE

### What is a procedure?

Procedures are a process or method implemented to define a specific instruction necessary to perform a task..

**Why to create a policy and procedures manual?**

A policy and procedures manual is one of the most important documents you can create for yourself and your employees. This document will help you manage your company and expect anticipated results from your employees and customers. It helps to define what you expect from your employees and what your employees expect from your company and you.

Your policy and procedures will give you insights on how decisions are made, how work is done, how to consistently do things to get the same results every time. A policy and procedures manual also helps with accountability and transparency.

**How to write a policy and procedure manual?**

If you are starting a business you do not need an elaborate policy and procedures manual. You can write down how you would like to see your organization's work in few pages. Once your company grows and you have more employees you will definitely need a thorough policy and procedures manual.

**When you are developing your policy and procedures manual you need to cover the following:**

a. Accounting:

When and how to pay bills? On which day payroll will be? When will financial reports be prepared? and so on.

b. Employee: What is your policy and procedures for employee's vacation and sick days? What time should employees report to work and when are the breaks and lunch breaks scheduled?

c. Work Performance and job promotion: What is the policy for job evaluation and promotions?

d. Policy for marketing and sales

e. Policy for customer service

f. Policy for shipping and delivery.

**Job Description:**

A job description requires a clear outline and explanation of the duties, responsibilities and qualifications for each position. You should have a job description for everyone from the secretary to the manager. Every job description needs to be customized to meet your company's needs.

*"It does not matter how slowly you go as long as you do not stop".*

*-Confucius*

# Chapter-17

# Time Management

**HOW TO GET DONE IN LESS TIME?**

*"You get to decide where your time goes, you can either spend it in moving forward or you can spend it putting out fires. You decide and if you do not decide others will decide for you."*

-Tony Morgan

**What is time management?**

A definition by Free-Time-Management-Tips.com is well presented.

Time Management is the art of arranging your business and personal affairs in such a way that you and your things show up when, where and how you intended them to, as frequently, effortlessly and ubiquitously as possible to facilitate getting things done as quickly as possible with the least amount of resources, time, energy, money and people necessary.

**Why time management is so important?**

Time management teaches you how to manage your time effectively and make the most of it. If you have good time management skills, you can get things done in less time. You can do more quality work, keep on track and stay disciplined. When you get things done in a timely fashion, you have time for family and for socializing. Last but not the least you have control over your life. If you set up good time management practices in your life, you will be working smarter not harder. Good time management will reduce your stress.

**Tips for time management:**

-Plan your day. Write out what tasks you want to accomplish and how long they should take you.

-At the end of each day, review your daily planner or to do list. Whatever you did not get done, put it on the next day.

-Delegate some of your work to your teammates.

-Learn to say "No" to those who steal your time.

-Categorize your to-do-list in order of importance: Work which will generate revenue, work which has deadlines or work that produces results.

-Find out where your time is being wasted and fix that problem.

-Evaluate your time management periodically and see where you can make improvements.

-Limit distractions.

-Set aside time for exercise, relaxation, eating well, spending time with family, socializing and getting a good night sleep.

-Think of your time in terms of money. Think of your time as being worth $1000/hour and work accordingly.

-Working longer does not mean being more productive.

-Organize meetings only when necessary and in the morning. Keep meetings focused and to the point.

-If you are in sales, use 90% of your time selling.

-Think only about today or tomorrow.

-Have a deadline for every important task.

-Work on one thing at a time. Multi-tasking is not always good.

-Try and reduce procrastination tendencies.

-Set up your long term planner.

-Have your time clock where you can see the time.

-Leave some buffer time in between.


*"Do not behold by the calendar there are only as many days in the year as you make use of. One man gets only a weeks value out of a year while another man gets a full years value out of a week."*

*-Charles Richards*

# Chapter-18

# The Profit

*"Profit in business comes form repeat customers, customers that boast about your product and service and that bring friends with them"*

*-W. Edwards Deming*

Profit is the money a business makes after deducting all the expenses.

You as the owner will need to determine how your company will generate income and create profit. Whether you are a one man operation or a large corporation, you have to find a way to make a profit. If there is no profit, there will be no business. So your goal is to keep expenses low and keep gross sales high to generate profit.

**All the income - All the expense = Profit**

or

**Gross sale - Cost of goods sold = Gross Profit**

**How to get net profit:**

**Gross profit – Operating expense = Net Profit**

You can set up an accounting system to get a monthly report on your net profit. As a business owner you need to know your net profit.

**Importance of Profit**

1. New businesses need money to get started. Machinery, equipment, furniture, fixtures and a lease on a space; these expenses are known as the initial cost.

2. All businesses must pay operating costs, such as rent, utilities, wages and delivery of goods. This is called operating expenses.

The gross profit is not the final profit. It is the profit after the cost of goods. Gross profit minus the operating cost of running the business is the net profit.

Every business hopes, in the end, they will make a profit, but few make it a measure of success. Profit is what you gain for the ideas, talent and hard work that you bring to make your business a success. Many times people focus on growing their business, but any growth without a profit is more work. In other words, revenue without profit is simply hard work for nothing. You must set up a profit goal and grow your business with profits. A profit is a measure of your success, a return on your investment, if you will. Profit is how you build a successful business. It is more than a job. You must make a bigger profit than you would from a fair market salary if you were working in the same job. This should be your primary goal for the immediate and long term future of your business.

To conclude understand the importance of

A. Gross Income or Revenue.

B. Cost of Goods Sold.

C. Gross Profit

D. Operating Cost.

E. Net profit or Net Income*

* Net Income is profit before taxes. You will still have to pay taxes on this income depending on your income bracket.

*"Be who you are and say what you feel, because those who mind do not matter and those who matter do not mind"*

-Bernard M Baruch

# Chapter-19

# In Closing

*"Every great dream begins with a dreamer, always remember you have within you the strength, the patience and the passion to reach the stars and change the world"*

-Harriet Tubman

Now comes the hard part, taking the first step towards starting your business. You may have both positive and negative thoughts: excitement, doubts, joy, fears and a multitude of varying emotions. Just remember, thought comes and goes, waxing and waning like the tide. It is important to control your thoughts and stay focused about starting your business.

**Here are 7 steps which will help you to move forward with your own plan and succeed.**

1. Conquer fears

2. Stay positive

3. Thought power

4. Will power

5. Passion

6. Commitment

7. Courage

**1. Conquer Fear:**

Fear is crippling. You need to conquer your fears. Both the fear of failure and the fear of maintaining success needs to be handled. Once you develop confidence in your ability to overcome your fears, your fears will gradually disappear. Have faith in yourself, nothing can stop you from reaching your goals.

**2. Stay Positive:**

Think positively. Have a positive attitude about you and your business. It may be helpful to read books on maintaining positive thoughts, listening an encouraging audio books, watching inspiring videos. Keep up-beats about your plan. Remember positive energy generates positive results, negative energy generates negative results. Thus, it is important to stay positive.

**3. Thought Power:**

Each thought you have creates energy within you and around you. Control your thoughts and have a clear vision. Set aside some quiet time for yourself to get your thoughts clear and think about your desire to succeed in your business. Think it, feel it, believe it. What you think of all day long is what you become. Ultimately, you are your thoughts.

-Your thoughts become your words

-Your words become your actions

-Your actions become your habits

-Your habits becomes your character

-Your character becomes your destiny

*Therefore, control your thoughts.*

### 4. Will Power:

You must have will power, it does not matter how fierce the storm is, you need to weather it out. You need enduring strength, energy, stamina, toughness and tenacity- the power to withstand hardship and stress and not give up. Survival will be the key, so cultivate will power.

### 5. Passion:

Passion is an intense emotion about your business. Your passion will generate enthusiasm, determination, strength and an unwavering desire to succeed. So be passionate about your business. Feel the excitement about your plan. Start doing what you love and enjoy.

## 6. Commitment:

You must be committed to your business and its success. Your commitment to your business, your employees, your customers is critical. Your new business will require your single-minded devotion. The outcome of your new business is ultimately your responsibility.

## 7. Courage:

You need courage to start your business. Do what you love and what you are passionate about. Courage is not only about physical bravery, being an entrepreneur takes incredible courage. Taking financial risks to follow your dream and change the world is not for the faint of heart.

Lastly, It does not matter how smart you are or how much experience you have, I truly believe that if you follow these seven principles you will succeed.

I hope this book will encourage you to take the next step and find your path to success. My love and best wishes are always with you.

*"Do not wait for extraordinary opportunities, seize common occasions and make them great"*

-Orison Swett Marden